the MONEY QUEEN'S GUIDE

the MONEY QUEEN'S GUIDE

*For Women Who Want to
Build Wealth and Banish Fear*

CARY CARBONARO, CFP®, MBA

New York

the MONEY QUEEN'S GUIDE

For Women Who Want to Build Wealth and Banish Fear

Published in New York, New York, by Morgan James Publishing. Morgan James and The Entrepreneurial Publisher are trademarks of Morgan James, LLC.
www.MorganJamesPublishing.com

The Morgan James Speakers Group can bring authors to your live event. For more information or to book an event visit The Morgan James Speakers Group at
www.TheMorganJamesSpeakersGroup.com.

A **free** eBook edition is available with the purchase of this print book.

CLEARLY PRINT YOUR NAME ABOVE IN UPPER CASE

Instructions to claim your free eBook edition:
1. Download the BitLit app for Android or iOS
2. Write your name in **UPPER CASE** on the line
3. Use the BitLit app to submit a photo
4. Download your eBook to any device

ISBN 978-1-63047-557-4 paperback
ISBN 978-1-63047-558-1 eBook
Library of Congress Control Number:
2015901024

Cover Design by:
Rachel Lopez
www.r2cdesign.com

Interior Design by:
Bonnie Bushman
bonnie@caboodlegraphics.com

In an effort to support local communities and raise awareness and funds, Morgan James Publishing donates a percentage of all book sales for the life of each book to Habitat for Humanity Peninsula and Greater Williamsburg.

Get involved today, visit
www.MorganJamesBuilds.com

Habitat
for Humanity®
Peninsula and
Greater Williamsburg
Building Partner

DEDICATION

I dedicate this book to my dad, Paul F. Carbonaro. He was a leader who inspired others and would light up the room with his smile. He instilled hard working values and to always be kind, fair and treat everyone with love and respect. He told me you can do anything you want in life and also taught me everything about money. My goal is to be a living legend for him.

This book is also dedicated to Stephen Leeds, my amazing husband who supports me in every way. He is my true partner and the love of my life. He makes me better person and I could not imagine my life without the light in his eyes.

TABLE OF CONTENTS

Acknowledgments

Thanks to Jessica Bellucci, Jarett Bellucci, Barbara Golemme, Matt Leeds, Michael Duncan, Richard Westhelle, Dawn Robertson, JJ Dahl, Justin Spitzman, Julie Barer, Susan Golomb, Abby Koons, Dennis Nelson, Jacqueline Stevenson, Erin Catherine, Kathleen Hands and all my amazing family, friends and clients!

DEAR READER

Dear Reader,

In one way or another, we are all driven by money. Male, female, young and old, we have all been told, trained, educated, and sold the notion that money is pretty important. It opens doors, creates opportunity, generates freedom, and offers us the exciting ability to create the life we want. We all have a relationship with it. Some of us have a healthy one, and others do not. But so long as we live, money is relevant and apparent around us. We cannot survive without it and it is ingrained in our minds that we should acquire as much of it as possible. Because you never know when you will have a rainy day, or just want to travel to a beautiful island that is not so rainy. Good, bad, or indifferent, money is one heck of a driving force that we have to recognize and discuss.

As much as we are motivated to make money, we often do not consider the crucial relationship between what we do today and how it can impact our life tomorrow. Every dollar we save and every dollar we spend has a meaningful impact on our financial stability and security as we age. But rarely do we consider this connection when we buy that car, or take that trip, or purchase that house. We often justify careless and wasteful spending with the notion that we have the rest of our lives to save and make adult decisions.

But I am here to help you think mindfully about the choices you make. My entire life has been driven by a need to help people, specifically women. As a Certified Financial Planner for over twenty years, I have seen it all. The ups, the downs, and even the lefts and the rights. As women, we are pulled in every direction imaginable. We fight to create a career, to give birth and then parent children. Instead of relying upon others, I want you to develop a financially independent lifestyle. Over the course of my career, I view myself, and many of my clients, as what I like to call "Designer Bag Ladies." This term is one we will discuss throughout the book, but for starters, a Designer Bag Lady is a woman who is extremely successful but still has fears about money. We all know one of them. She may be our neighbor, our best friend, a loved one, or even a colleague a work. She is widely successful, has it all, but still feels the need for reassurance and constantly doubts her financial stability and earning abilities. It is truly the notion of a modern day woman. I consider myself to be, a Designer Bag Lady and "The Money Queen."

Throughout my own career, I have grown to see myself as more than a financial planner. I'm also a teacher, a therapist, and counselor who, every day, seeks to help clients, friends, and family with all sorts of money related issues. I have a desire to share the lessons I've learned through the years, not just the financial education I learned in college or the lessons learned through my professional development. I also get a great amount of satisfaction in sharing my life experiences—both the triumphs and the mistakes—in the hope that others will benefit from them, as well. In my mind, that's how the world turns. Sharing our experiences helps us to all become our best while learning to live a more authentic life.

This book not only outlines my own journey, but also discusses many of the topics and important money related issues we, as women, experience on a daily basis including the struggle, the fight, and the battle to manifest a healthy relationship with money. I remain a big proponent of counseling for all kinds of life's struggles. "Financial therapy" has become part of my own personal brand, as I saw how reconciling my emotions with my reality made for a better, stronger money mind. Through this journey, we will discuss money and the opportunity to make intelligent financial decisions through the course of your life, not just when you are at the end of your earning ability.

There are tried and true decisions you can make as early as your teens that can positively impact your financial security. It is pretty amazing that the manner in which you apply for student loans or the money earned from your college job can impact your ability to retire early. But it can and it does. Every dollar you don't spend now can turn into thousands of dollars you don't have to earn later. As you travel through this book, you will quickly see that your twenties, thirties, forties, fifties, and sixties all present decade specific challenges and exciting opportunities to build a financially thoughtful life. So we will take it ten years at a time.

The goal is not to overwhelm, but to provide you with clear and concise steps you can take to truly position yourself for financial independence. Life can be tricky, complicated, and sometimes really, really expensive. But if you weather the storm early, you will be better situated to manage what is to come. Every dollar earned is an opportunity and a building block for your future. And through my lessons, and mistakes, I am confident that together we can journey to a place of financial stability that starts now and ends sooner than you think.

Money Queen Fact: 42% of all women lack financial security.[1]

Chapter 1

ARE YOU A MATERIAL GIRL?

Money. The Bible tells us, "It's the root of all evil." Benjamin Franklin said, "Money has never made man happy, nor will it, there is nothing in its nature to produce happiness. The more of it one has the more one wants." Margaret Thatcher reminded us, "It is not the creation of wealth that is wrong, but the love of money for its own sake." Voltaire said, "Don't think money does everything or you are going to end up doing everything for money." Sound pretty disconcerting?

But then we remember when Rita Davenport said, "Money isn't everything…but it ranks right up there with oxygen." Or when Groucho Marx said, "While money can't buy happiness, it certainly lets you choose your own form of misery." And then there was Jim Young, played by Ben Affleck, in the movie *Boiler Room*, who said, "Anybody who tells you money is the root of all evil doesn't have any.

They say money can't buy happiness? Look at the smile on my face. Ear to ear, baby." We can all agree there are some pretty conflicting views on money.

Needless to say, money is one hot topic that has built quite the reputation as time goes on. It is something for which we strive and for which we yearn. It is something we acquire and then divest and invest into other things. Sometimes we hold onto it for an extended period while other times it leaves us as quickly as we earned it. We all know someone who cannot save a dollar no matter how much she makes. And then there is that friend in our circle who saves every dollar she earns. Most people feel the wealthiest folks are those that make the most money. And maybe they are. But the reality is that the wealthiest people in this world not only make the most money, but also save and invest the most money. It is pretty darn easy to be rich today and poor tomorrow. No matter how much you make, if you spend it all, there will be little, if any, left.

But that practice is generally the exception, not the rule, especially for women. Many times, young women are raised to be dependent upon men, rarely armed with the extensive knowledge they need to not only earn money, but also be self-sufficient and save it. We are told that we will always be supported and prince charming will always provide for all of our financial needs. I don't believe in this fairy tale. Women are just as capable as men of taking care of themselves and their finances. The truth is that as women, we are independent and able to support ourselves. In fact, it is our duty to be responsible for ourselves both personally and professionally.

Money Queen Fact: According to the 2009 U.S. Bureau of Labor Statistics, nearly 4 in 10 working wives out earned their husbands.

But remember when I told you we would learn from my mistakes? Well my first mistake was undertaking the difficult task of supporting myself and my husband as the financial breadwinner. When it all fell apart, every decision I made during our marriage positioned me for economic destruction. The truth is that I was so fearful of becoming dependent on others that I picked an emotionally unavailable man who I only connected with on a surface level. In fact, my father jokingly said we exchanged resumes and he looked good on paper. It was never a fairy tale love story. It was the easy way out. He was good looking, smart and successful. But, ultimately, he was the wrong man for the wrong reasons. But funny enough, my journey was one that paralleled so many other women of the world.

Independent Woman

Like many modern day women, I came from a very traditional household. Growing up watching the dynamic of my mom and dad, I decided I wanted to be more like my dad…I wanted to be the one who made the money.

My story is similar to that of many women; I've had some great successes, great failures, and I've had to re-chart my financial life in the face of change more than once. I'm human, just like everyone else. I built a successful business, got married, experienced a painful and financially damaging divorce, and then had to rebuild. But I've also followed my passions throughout life. One of those passions is financial planning. As a child, my banker father exposed me early on to the financial world. He taught me strong money values, the importance of working hard, and gave me my love for doing the right things with money. His bank often hosted "Take your Daughter to Work" days, and I was front and center at every one. My mother was a big part of that passion, too. She is a Certified Public

Accountant, and she also went back to school later in life, when I was 13.

Money Queen Fact: 90% of women believe they need to be involved in the financial planning process.[2]

After graduating from college, my career moved quickly up the corporate ladder, including eight years on Wall Street at *JP Morgan Chase*, three years as a Vice President at *Citibank*, and two years as a Director at *Lord Abbett Investments*. By the time I turned 30, I was earning $500,000 a year. I'm not going to lie: I thought I had it made! I had met and exceeded so many goals in life. What could possibly go wrong? I was clearly financial independent with that much money coming in every year. Or so I thought. I was confident in my ability to support myself. I refused to learn normal domestic duties because I had determined that would not be for me. I thought: *If I make the money, then I will be safe, be able to make my own decisions, and have freedom.*

That line of thinking is nearly always a preamble for disaster. And it demonstrates much of what occurs to us. As women, we often set ourselves up for failure. Whether we knew it at the time or not, the writing was always on the wall. Life takes us to unexpected places all the time. In my case, it led me into a romantic relationship that, in the end, caused major negative effects on my happiness, my confidence, and my financial bottom line. I made the wrong choice in my life because of my unhealthy emotional state. It wasn't for lack of intellect or knowledge. In fact, most bad decisions are driven out of either conscious or unconscious emotional responses.

In 2000, I married someone who I thought I could be coupled with. He was a CPA and an attorney with an impressive resume. I felt as if we were both at the same point on the fast track. He was what I wanted and, on paper, it was a perfect merger of equals...or at least that's what

I thought. But boy was I wrong and the cost was unbelievable and immeasurable. In the end, money was the least of my worries.

Money Can't Buy Me Love

When I entered into marriage, I had no idea what I was in for. I was open, vulnerable and trusting, which made me the perfect victim. Sounds familiar, doesn't it? All the while, I carried the bulk of our shared financial burden. I had come into the marriage as the primary breadwinner, and that showed no signs of changing any time soon. I always paid my own bills, so at first, I didn't realize I was paying for nearly everything. Bills came in and my income went out. I just paid ALL the bills. We never had joint banking accounts. He had his money and I had mine. I thought that would protect me. My name appeared on the bills as they came in and I paid them because it was my responsibility. Or at least that was how I viewed it.

My husband had his own reasons for not chipping in. He referred to himself as a "serial entrepreneur," who would never work for anyone other than himself. He was stubborn, unwilling to undertake traditional work, and completely attached to my ability to pay for it all. He said he was an ex-hedge fund manager who had retired twice by the time he was 30. His money was his, and was "unavailable" for paying bills. I also soon realized that his finances were a mess. On the surface, he was successful and well-to-do, but scratch the surface and he had terrible credit. He'd never paid back his undergraduate or law school student loans. He had accounts under his control in his father's name, his mother's, and even an old girlfriend's name, in which he would sock money away. He had more than a dozen companies set up in his name, creating such a quagmire around tax time that his files would arrive in a box nearly as tall as me. It was impossible for me to figure out what was going on with his money, but he always seemed to know what was going on with mine. I simply accepted his lies and wrote the checks because I was taught to always be responsible and pay the bills on time. My stellar credit rating was very important to me and he knew it.

Not long after our move to Florida from New York, my father passed away. The ground slipped out from under my feet and I was spinning out of control. Looking back, I can say with some certainty that this time in my life was my rock bottom.

I'd started a new financial practice, but my marriage was still in decline. When the divorce began, money was literally flying out the window as quick as it came in the door. Ultimately, I found myself on a long, lonely road to divorce. It was a process that lasted for years and included countless contract negotiations and financial red tape that threatened not just my earnings to date, but my future earnings as well. Once the relationship ended, the financial conundrum began. My ex-husband felt he was entitled to much of what I earned and almost all that I built. Never mind you that I made most of the money and paid the bills. That was not enough. He wanted it all. And worst of all, he felt that it was his right.

It was an arduous, six-figure divorce with emotionally driven decisions affecting me at every turn. I owned two houses, but while the titles of those homes were in both our names, the mortgages were in my name alone. This meant that, for a long time, my ex was living in one of those homes while I paid the mortgage, bills, and car payments. He was living the dream while I was trapped in an emotional and financial nightmare. Relief was nowhere to be found.

Anyone who knew me asked: *"Why would you do that?"* The short answer is that emotions were fueling my decisions. Of course, it's never as simple as that—emotions never are. For one, I had fabulous credit and, as taught by my parents, felt driven to pay every bill for which I was responsible, fair or not. I knew that in the long run, I would be punished if I didn't pay the bills.

One of my biggest reasons for staying as long as I did was fear. It wasn't just the threats my husband levied against me, but I was afraid of losing everything I'd built. The only thing I did still have control over was my business. I'd created it and watched it start to thrive in spite of everything that was happening in my own life. It became my lifeboat, so I started to think that if I could get to a certain benchmark in my career, I could make things start to happen in my personal life. *When I make X,* I'd reason with myself, *I'll walk away.*

---

*Money Queen Fact: 49% of women fear
losing all of their money and becoming homeless.*[3]

One day, I was presented out of the blue with a Marital Separation Agreement that my husband had drafted completely on his own. When I arrived at home, I was ambushed with six witnesses waiting for me to sign a 100-page document that I'd never seen before. After reading only six pages, I realized the agreement stipulated I hand over 50% of my business…the only thing I knew I had control over that was 100% my own. The rest of the day turned into a blur as I was bullied into signing the document through verbal abuse and threats. My professional side knew something was very wrong, but the emotional toll of the situation was just too much for me to take. I signed the agreement under duress. I literally gave away half of what I earned and half of what I had worked tirelessly to build. Through my signature, it was his.

For weeks, he and his staff refused to provide me a copy. When I finally received a copy of the agreement, I went to see a dear trusted friend, who is also a Board Certified family-law attorney. We reviewed the entire agreement and found that not only did it ask me to sacrifice half of my business, but it also appointed my ex-husband as executor of my estate—he was to receive 50% of my future inheritances, and many more stipulations that, in hindsight, were crazy. If I violated any stipulation, including moving my business, the "agreement" stated I would owe him five million dollars in a "liquidated damages clause." On top of everything else, as soon as divorce proceedings started I was sued for alimony and temporary support. It was literally a one-sided financial catastrophe.

After endless tears, my friend offered a glimmer of hope. She said the document was so egregious that she didn't believe it would hold up in court. It was clear to any unbiased bystander that I was manipulated and coerced into signing the agreement. I hired an attorney and prepared for battle—the ultimate battle. During the divorce, I was bleeding cash. I could not make money fast enough and I was in the red every month for the first time in my entire life. I was fortunate to have an emergency fund, something I advise all of my clients to have, and it allowed me to get though the almost four years of negative cash flow. This was the first glimpse of a silver lining I had after years of bad tidings. It even gave me a little chuckle, reminding me of a quote from one of my favorite movies, *It's a Wonderful Life*. Annie, the Bailey's housekeeper, gives George some of her hard-earned cash at the close of the film and says, "I've been savin' this money for a divorce, if ever I got a husband!" But I was determined to put my head down, suck it up, and stand strong to ensure I stood for what I believed. I didn't deserve this treatment and I was the victim. It was time I fought hard to protect what I built over the first half of my life. I was a powerful woman, but this man would try to take everything away from me. I had to literally fight for my life.

I Will Survive

Throughout my personal struggles, financial planning remained a professional endeavor that brought me joy. It was a safe haven for me, and always put a smile on my face. It was as if I was living vicariously through the intelligent financial decisions of others. I was paying for my mistakes, but at least I was helping others. It all felt worth it. So I refocused on my job and found new aspects of the industry that made me happy. After years of struggle, as well as personal development, I was ready to take my life to its highest and best use. My personal trials and tribulations could only be fantastic examples and learning experiences for others.

Many of my bad decisions came in the form of my taste in men. My Achilles heel was intimate relationships. I was simply attracted to the wrong type of guy. I had a wonderful role model in my dad, why should I keep making poor decisions in this area of my life? I explored this for years in my counseling sessions. When I first started, my counselor asked me, "What do you feel?" I didn't even understand the question. I was so out of touch with my emotional being, which I deemed to be too female, that I didn't know what I didn't know.

How could I choose the right partner when I didn't even know how to emotionally relate? This took years of peeling back the onion, layer after layer. It was hard work and I always wanted to quit. My therapist would say, "Cary, I am committed to you, you have to be committed to me. This is your life we are saving." I had already been burned badly. I was still trying to put the pieces of my life back together. My life was damaged and my business was damaged.

And then came a glimmer of light at the end of the dark tunnel. I was at the Orlando airport one Monday morning in late 2009 when I struck up a conversation with a man in the security line. This wasn't unusual. I often start conversations with people around me, and didn't think much of it. But by the end of the line, I knew he was from Long Island just like me and also lived in Central Florida, just like me. He worked in both states and was a professional in the pharmaceutical industry. He also had experienced a very difficult and contentious divorce.

We exchanged emails and phone numbers and contact info after talking for a long time. He emailed me the next day and asked if I wanted to go out for coffee, lunch, or dinner in Florida or New York. He said it was my choice. He wanted to give me options! I really wasn't sure if I should accept...I didn't think I was ready to let another man into my life. To be completely cautious and not rush into another relationship, I kept my distance and allowed our friendship to grow.

We communicated via email over the next few months. He had such a positive outlook on life, with an amazing spirit, and a genuine smile that reached his eyes. He was very confident in himself and he knew who he was. It was extremely refreshing. When I told my therapist I wasn't sure I was ready to date, he told me to give him his number so he could reach out and speak with my new interest. I was terrified, but I did it. They spoke for an hour and a half. My therapist called me afterwards and told me, "This is the man I have always wanted for you—a true partner. You can give and receive love to each other." I felt relieved and was excited that I was able to filter through the crap and find a man that could potentially be a healthy fit in my life. I was seeing spots after my last relationship, so I was unsure if I could ever focus again. So it was with great enthusiasm that I began the process of opening my life to this man.

As our life blossomed together, I began to take a very reflective and strong look at my life up to that point. I quickly began to recognize that many, if not all, of my poor financial decisions were directly related to the opposite sex. My relationships directly led to much of the financial hardships I experienced.

That may be the first and most important lesson I can impart on you: don't allow your emotions to control your financial decisions. It is simply a recipe for disaster. I lost hundreds of thousands of dollars because I couldn't see that my emotional relationship was manifesting bad financial practices in my monetary relationship. This could have all been avoided if I simply opened my eyes. This is a common story for many women. We are emotional beings and we often lead with our emotions, allowing us to trust people we otherwise would not. And the result can be debilitating.

Inevitably, at some point in your life the line between personal decisions and financial decisions is going to blur…this was definitely a blurry time for me. The emotions were heavy and real, and they made it that much more difficult to see the forest from the trees, as the saying goes. This dichotomy of the head and the heart is the root cause of many poor financial decisions, and I was not immune. I lived it, and the silver lining is that I have learned to use those experiences to help others now that I've made it through the worst.

I was not your typical woman who was worried about ending up penniless. I was an educated, successful, self-sufficient woman of means who had designer bags, shoes, etc. My therapist said it was a dichotomy he thought was funny. He called me the Designer Bag Lady. I loved the name and so it stuck. I knew I was not alone when Allianz came out with the study that 27% of women who made over 200K had the same issue. Thus I gave birth to the term "Designer Bag Ladies." My clients love to say aloud, "I am the Designer Bag Lady." They call me and ask me if they can afford a new car or house. They admit their fear keeps them from being able to spend money even though they are successful and have more than enough. They quickly become their own worst enemy.

Women Empowering Women

So, where do we go from here? To start, women should be empowered and uplifted to begin the process of saving at an early age. It is not just about avoiding financial landmines as you age. It is also about being able to recover if you do step on one. My financial landmine was marrying a man and allowing him to syphon off much of what I worked hard to build. He was not entitled to it and did not deserve it. But I was manipulated and could not get out of the way of my own emotions. The important thing is to understand that if you save now, you will be positioned to absorb whatever life throws your way. I recovered and made it out of that relationship in one piece because I had the padding we all should have. For all of us, it has to start at an early age.

Beginning in your 20's, there is valuable information to gain and steps you can take to start the road to financial security. As each decade of your life passes, there are different management and saving plans that should be considered and incorporated. Building a nest egg and producing financial security does not happen overnight. It takes years of smart decisions and meticulous planning to be in a position of financial security. And even then one large tidal wave can knock down your strongly built foundation. So it makes it all the more important to take the steps now to plan for later.

I noticed a lot of my friends had fear and trepidation about finances that I didn't have, because I was taught how to work with money early on. These were smart women, who were feeling dumb about money! These were bright, accomplished young women with great futures ahead of them; yet, some didn't know how to establish a savings account never mind balance a checkbook! Worse, even if they did know where to turn for help, a lot of them were scared to try. Would they know the right questions to ask? Would they sound stupid? Would someone lead them down the wrong road?

Let's be honest, we are all material girls in some manner. Most of us enjoy a nice meal, or a beautiful new dress, or those gorgeous Italian heels. And the world around us supports this notion of consumerism. They want us to buy. They want us to apply for credit cards with large limits that we may or may not be able to afford. It sure is tough to save in this world. Saving isn't cool, but it is necessary. Because the stress you cause by not saving is far greater than the stress you experience by not having. I always say that not making that purchase today will yield you ten times that purchase some time in the future.

Financial Therapy: Admitting You Have a Problem

As women, we truly experience a unique set of circumstances in our financial lives. We are often spoon fed the notion that we should rely on our partners for financial support while simultaneously being told how important it is to have the most expensive makeup, clothes, purses, car, and house. We are constantly sold an ideal way of life— one that is consumer driven and completely reliant on our ability to spend. The result is we are blinded by what we see around us. We make bad financial decisions for no other reason than we feel it is the socially acceptable thing to do. The fallout can be great. And the worst part is we did it to ourselves.

The idea of financial therapy isn't just a buzz term. These days, it's on the top of my list of client services. It's offered at one time or another to nearly everyone who walks through my office doors…or who asks me out for lunch, or sits next to me on a plane, etc.

The reason is simple: As a society, we just haven't been taught to talk about money, or to separate emotional decisions from prudent decisions. That means a huge part of my job is constantly trying to get my clients to make better financial decisions during emotional times.

Usually, that means taking the heart out of the equation. Easier said than done, right?

For example, a successful woman might want to buy her dream home nestled on the water. She thinks she can afford it. She has enough money to buy the house, but that would be it. Her retirement fund would be gone, and living in that house may quickly become uncomfortable, if not impossible. All too many people find themselves in this situation, unable to see past the SOLD sign in front of that beachfront home. The self-gratification quickly wears off and is replaced with self-humiliation when she realizes she is living in a house she cannot afford.

> **Money Queen Fact:** *In 2004, the median income for retired women was $12,080 compared to $21,102 for men.*[4]

We all need to make sure we're taking our dreams past the instant gratification stage: past that sign, through the front door, and into the years that will follow. It all begins with a hard look inward. To embark on any plan, you should first be real and honest with yourself. You need to know who you are, and where you are going.

Everyone approaches money with three specific *emotionally rooted* drivers in mind: Commitment, fear, and happiness. We all have traits from each category, but usually, one comes more naturally to us than the others. To that end, let's discuss each of these so you can better understand how they interact with your financial situation:

Commitment: Are you driven by a sense to provide for your family?
Fear: Are you afraid you will run out or never have enough?
Happiness: Are you driven by a desire to have everything you want immediately because it makes you happy?

The firm I work for has an online quiz you can take to determine your Money Mind™. You can find it at http://findyourmoneymind.com. The results of this quiz will help you determine your "Money Mind™," and it becomes the basis for all sorts of financial conversations. Before I meet with a potential client, I ask her to take some time to identify her Money Mind™ through a series of questions rooted in real life situations. I ask questions such as, *"You've been offered a job across the country. What's your first thought?"* Questions like these help us to gauge our natural tendencies toward spending.

Not surprisingly, most of the world has a fear-based mindset when it comes to money. We are scared of the relationship, fearful of saving, fearful of spending, and therefore, simply brush it under the rug. For example, among women ages 35 to 49, 60% fall into the "fear" category, driven by a need for security and peace of mind. Fear focus isn't entirely negative; those who fall into this category are often cautious, careful decision makers who live within their means and are well prepared for the unexpected.

However, they also tend to be slow in making decisions at times, can experience anxiety when facing big financial commitments, and will make personal sacrifices to maintain their overall financial security. You probably have a friend or family member who fits the bill: those who would hide their assets under the mattress if they could. In today's world, that drive to squirrel away money in a safe place might mean these types would be comfortable with stable portfolios that can weather the market's ups and downs. These women are the ones most likely to be my "bag ladies." If they are more financially successful women, then they are my "Designer Bag Ladies."

Someone with a "commitment mindset" is focused on taking care of others. They're excellent providers and consider the perspective of other people, not only when it comes to fulfilling obligations, but also in terms of how others will be affected by decisions they might make.

That said, they might put other people's needs ahead of their own. When working with a commitment mind, I try to ensure that all of their ducks are in a row in terms of long-term planning and paperwork. Life insurance, retirement plans, and other future needs are taken care of right away, so we can center our efforts on finding balance.

Money Queen Fact: 65% of women expect they will need to work longer and postpone retirement.[5]

Finally, women with a "happiness mind" are focused on the here and now. They're decisive, even with big decisions, and tend not to dwell on potential problems in the future. They often feel as if they don't have enough, though, and can over-emphasize instant gratification; credit card debt can be a particular problem. They may have little in savings and usually haven't planned for when things aren't going well. A happiness-focused person might benefit from less traditional savings plans, like flexible spending packages and automatic deposits into 401(k) plans or Roth IRAs. Essentially, people with a happiness mindset need to have savings put on autopilot for them because it's just not their first priority.

Based on these descriptions, you probably already have an idea of where your tendencies lie. Keep them in mind, along with your dreams for the future, when building your plan. It's just one of many tools that help to keep us focused on the rewards ahead. You may even find that you do not squarely fit into one single category. Some people demonstrate qualities and characteristics from two, if not all three, of the categories. The purpose of considering where you fall is to help gain a better understanding of your tendencies and historical behaviors when it comes to finances. Through acknowledging your trends, you can consider which ones should be celebrated and which ones can be changed. Building a life with financial security is an ever-changing and moving target. What works today may be a recipe for disaster tomorrow. So, it is important to consistently be aware and cognizant of who you are and where your tendencies fall.

Chapter 2

THE FIVE KEYS TO FINANCIAL PLANNING

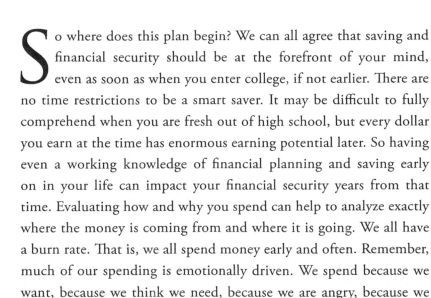

So where does this plan begin? We can all agree that saving and financial security should be at the forefront of your mind, even as soon as when you enter college, if not earlier. There are no time restrictions to be a smart saver. It may be difficult to fully comprehend when you are fresh out of high school, but every dollar you earn at the time has enormous earning potential later. So having even a working knowledge of financial planning and saving early on in your life can impact your financial security years from that time. Evaluating how and why you spend can help to analyze exactly where the money is coming from and where it is going. We all have a burn rate. That is, we all spend money early and often. Remember, much of our spending is emotionally driven. We spend because we want, because we think we need, because we are angry, because we are celebrating, and because it is advertised to do so. At the core of each of these behaviors are our emotions. Emotion driven spending is surely a recipe for a disastrous result.

Emotions impact all of us. It is our human nature and simply impossible to separate our emotions from our behaviors. But we can work to ensure our decisions are not driven by our emotions. When it comes to money, making emotional decisions is a trend that binds us all together. Emotions don't discriminate based on the size of your net worth. If there's one thing I've learned, and that I pass on to nearly everyone I meet, it's the simple truth that no one has ever made a poor financial decision without emotions being part of the mix. They may have played a small role, or even a larger one, but regardless, they are always involved. Whether it's anger, happiness, greed, fear, or any combination of these, it's our feelings that derail us and position us for a great demise.

Emotional Decisions

Emotional decisions—whether based happiness, fear, or another feeling—occur at every stage of life. Even as we become more connected and in control of our emotions, we will never be fully capable of removing them from the equation. So what can you do to minimize the role emotions play in your financial decisions? There is not one right answer. It will always change. The answer when you're in college is different than the answer when you enter the real world and begin your career, or when you're getting married, or if you're getting divorced. Further, emotional decisions are sometimes even more clouded by a lack of information. Enormous emotions combined with bad information are almost certainly a disaster waiting to happen.

Later in life, after careers have been forged and investments made, emotional decisions persist. Knowing you're on the right track and having someone guide you can make all the difference. The lessons presented in the forthcoming pages will help you make the right decisions related to money in all the stages and transitions of your life. Education, experience and therapy have helped me be a rock for my clients. I remain a big proponent of counseling for all kinds of life's struggles and "financial therapy" has become part of my own personal brand, as I saw how reconciling my emotions with my reality made for a better, stronger money mind.

In fact counseling helps to squash those "bag lady" fears. Working with an unbiased, impartial and well-trained financial advisor can offer honest feedback for you to consider. I am not your typical woman worried about ending up penniless. I am an educated, successful, self-sufficient woman of means who definitely enjoys the finer things in life. The key is not to turn into a robot because emotions can help you make decisions. The important gift I would like to give to you is the valuable tips and tools you can use to create a separation between your emotions and your financial decisions. Emotions will always be a factor, but they should never be the driving force. I was often the victim of my emotions. I married the wrong man and allowed him to take advantage of me, and my hard work, every day of our marriage. But eventually, I took the emotions out of it, and recognized that if it were not for my emotions, I could have dodged this one. But the lessons I learned and the experience I had only further positioned me to ensure you do not make the same gigantic missteps.

Money Queen Fact: 36% of Financial Advisors are women.[6]
Only 23 percent of Certified Financial Planners are women

Five Keys to Financial Planning

At its best, proper financial planning can give you an enormously exciting opportunity to find financial freedom later in life. It allows you to do what you want, go where you want to go, and be a healthy consumer without limitation. Maybe you want to surprise your grandchild with a car when he turns sixteen, or take your family on a Caribbean cruise, or purchase a vacation home, or maybe even set up a college savings account for young children. Whatever the case may be, the options are endless if you are financially stable and work hard to responsibly save.

There are five keys to financial planning that can be revisited at any age and that will help to acquire the freedom to spend later. They are simple, straightforward, but extremely meaningful and powerful. If implemented into your daily financial decisions, they can slowly reinvent your journey to financial stability. Collectively, our goal together is to consider your planning goals and then make the decisions early in life that will help position you to reach them. It is not always easy, but with just a little discipline and thought, they are very much in play. These five important steps include:

1. Know your net worth. Your net worth is the calculation of your assets minus your current liabilities. Assets are anything you own like a car, a house, your stocks, bonds, or any other investment. Liabilities are what you owe like your mortgage, a car loan/lease, or debt like student loans or credit cards.

2. Know how you're doing. Consider questions like: How am I doing related to my peers? My age group? My income? Most times, a financial professional can help to give you an honest assessment of your current situation.

3. Keep on target to meet your goal. First you have to know what your goals are. Next, take the time to analyze and evaluate those goals as you move in their general (and eventually more specific) direction.

4. Have an advocate or coach to help you. There are an enormous amount of resources and people out there (like me) with specialized expertise that can help track your journey and

measure it as you go. Consider meeting with a few of them to determine who'd be the right fit for you.

5. Sleep better knowing you're financially secure. A financial advocate supporting you can help to make the journey significantly less stressful, and will help position you to sleep much better at night.

In other words, ask yourself the following:

What do I want to do?
Where do I want to go?
With whom do I want to take this journey?

The answers to these questions help point people toward experiences that are in line with their goals and with their budgets. Alignment is a crucial concept to recognize and understand. Magic can happen when our financial decisions align with our financial limitations. It is not easy. But boy can it be a difference maker. We'll keep revisiting those ideas throughout this book—they are just one tool that keeps us on track. But they are very important in the journey to financial stability. They reduce stress, they raise awareness, and they play pivotal roles in determining the level of security you can reach and at what age you can reach it. As you reduce stress, you minimize the role emotions may play in your decisions. While they do require dedication and determination and sensible decisions, the reward far outweighs the small amount of extended energy. You will find that if you are in a constant financial flux, you will run yourself rampant with lost opportunities and heartbreak through out your journey.

Based on the information provided up to this point, you may have already asked, *"When do I need a plan for my financial life?"* Regardless of your age, the answer to that question is **NOW**, and it's essential to achieving life goals at any stage. Remember, the sooner you start the journey, the sooner you will reach your destination. Financial planning has its rewards and some of the benefits (such as increases in your savings account) may be difficult to see at first. It is not always easy cutting back or passing on that trip or driving that older model of your car. But knowing you're on the right track, and taking advantage of some guidance along the way, makes a world of difference. If you make the right decisions now, there will always be an opportunity to reward yourself in the future with those things you sacrificed earlier in your life. But at the end of the day, I want to ease fears and provide guidance for all stages of life.

According to the 2013 Women, Money & Power Study from insurer Allianz Life, nearly half of all American women fear becoming a "bag lady." Such concerns aren't limited to people who are struggling financially: 27% of women earning more than $200,000 per year share that fear. The study found that anxiety about ending up broke is consistent across all types of women, with the highest for single respondents (56%). But, it is also a significant concern for divorced women (54%), widows (47%) and married women (43%). In short, it can impact us all in many different ways.

The bag lady fears persist, even as women are feeling better about their earning potential. But for most, the bag lady fear is purely emotional. By understanding the crux of the problem and evaluating its root case, we can empower women so they can squelch that fear with knowledge. And the first step in the journey is creating a strong game plan. This game plan will help you organize your financial road to success. As a huge fan of music and concerts (can't you tell by my quotes?), I look at financial planning like a band looks at a concert at a large venue. They wouldn't step on stage without rehearsals and an agreed upon list of songs they will play, also known as a "set." The same is true when planning for financial security. It is important to rehearse or practice throughout your life to ensure you are clear on what your "set" or game plan will look like. By outlining your parameters and journey, much like a band, you will be prepared to succeed and completely rock.

Money Queen Fact: There are 69 million women in the workforce; 10 million of them are their family's sole breadwinners.[7]

It should start early in your life and quietly grow to become an important and vital part of your existence. Understanding how current financial decisions can impact your ultimate goals later should become an important part of your life. It should be embedded in your soul and often at the forefront of your mind. Each and every day we plan vacations, dinners, birthday parties, and many other important events. They all carry value, but are merely a drop in the well of life. So if we plan so many of these moments, why do we often fall short when it comes to planning our financial security and future? We will discuss the emotions and basis for this behavior as we work towards building your ideal game plan. And once we do that, you will feel more equipped and well positioned to undertake this responsibility. I wouldn't refer to it as difficult. I would just say that it is a journey that requires thought, planning, and discipline. As you grow and mature, the necessity for saving will become more and more apparent. But it will also become entirely more challenging since your overall responsibilities will increase. But if you instill restraint and control at a younger age, you will find it easy to adjust those important habits as you grow personally and professionally.

Money Queen Fact: Only 23 percent of Certified Financial Planners are women[41]

Chapter 3

FAIL TO PLAN; PLAN TO FAIL

Would you take a long road trip without a map or directions? Would a pilot fly a plane without reviewing the weather forecast and planning the route? Would a construction company build a house without blueprints and planning? Would a teacher conduct a course in college without a curriculum? Would a rock band set foot onstage without a set? These are just a few examples, but we can all agree in each of these examples that the respective parties would invest some initial time into planning. Why? Well, because without planning, we are destined for failure. The house will crumble, the kids will not learn, and the concert will certainly not rock. After the soul-searching comes the planning stage. Some people are natural born planners. Schedules are made, routines are developed, and goals are set. But for others, planning doesn't always come so easily. Sure, you may be able to plan out what you're going to accomplish this week, but what about your future? What about the next year? Or five years? Or even ten years? Do you know where you want to be in 10 or 20 years down the line? Do you know what it will take to get you there? I am often met with a blank stare when I ask this question to my younger clients. It is just not something they have yet to consider.

Welcome to the world of financial planning, where your dreams come face-to-face with your financial reality. It starts with taking a look at where you are now, so you can start building towards your goals. Whether it's retirement, college tuition, or a tropical vacation— the fundamental principles that support the path to success are exactly the same. Of course, everyone is different. We all have our own fingerprints and personalities, our own style and our own way of thinking. It's no different for our outlook of the future—we all envision something different. But in today's world, obtaining your ideal future—at least when it comes to finances—has become increasingly daunting and often difficult. How do you live your own best financial life? Remember:

Financial planning isn't just for the very wealthy. There is valuable advice and guidance that can be shared during all parts of the journey. Financial planners are able to guide people from all walks of life through the, oftentimes, stressful and confusing world of finances. Sure, there's investing; but what about vacations? College? Weddings? Divorce? Retirement? Funerals? They all call for significant planning and thought. And most of us are not born with the training and skillset needed to properly manage our money. I know I didn't plan for much of my life. It took years of training, education, and learning from my mistakes, and the mistakes of others, before I truly felt comfortable enough to be a difference-maker in the lives of others.

But there is one thing we can mostly all agree on when it comes to financial planning: "if you do nothing, you'll get nothing."

The Devil is in the Details

When it comes to financial planning, the devil is truly in the details. From whom you choose to help with your journey, to how you take each step, your end result and success will ultimately be the culmination of each of these integral decisions. Consider the example of Lara. Two and a half years after her divorce was finalized, Lara still hadn't transferred her joint accounts, or those that were in her ex-husband's name, solely to her own name.

It wasn't apathy on her part. A settlement was reached after months of mediation, meetings with attorneys, and reams of paper work to sign, date, and deliver. It seemed as if the hardest part was behind her. She was simply exhausted. When it's all said and done, it's not really done; we can't expect financial transfers to happen on their own. Fees associated with old accounts could be accruing, assets could be missing, or new language may be required in the divorce papers. There are an enormous amount of loose ends that have to be addressed. After the trauma of divorce, many women have a fear of moving on because something else "might" happen. This situation is all too common among divorcees, and is just one example of how our emotions can interfere with our finances. So the result is that we allow these small concerns to fester, rarely addressing the outstanding issues. Ultimately, the simple act of not closing a bank account or transferring the couple hundred dollars left in a joint trust is not a big deal. But what does become a problem are the underlying habits or fundamental financial decisions that prevent you from doing so. Those are what need to be addressed and then changed.

Separation can impact every inch of your financial livelihood. Everything you built together has to now be disassembled so you can start afresh and rebuild. Once the divorce is over, you actually have to take action to transfer accounts into your name, get your former partner off the deed of the house, and remove him as your beneficiary, in addition to other financial steps to ensure the break is a clean one. These are some of the most important and overlooked steps. The attorney is usually not involved in this process. Rarely do you receive any independent advice to guide you through the loose ends that occur with divorce. You have to do it on your own or with a trusted advisor or financial planner, like myself. I have seen this take as long, or even longer, than the actual divorce to complete. Whether it is power of attorneys, numerous phone calls, visits to your local banks, or any other number of pieces of red tape through which you have to navigate, the road to post divorce financial independence can be tricky and very complicated.

After months or years of negotiations, that last bit of financial planning can feel like a mighty blow, but not moving forward soon after settlements are reached might result in losses of time, money, and patience. And that may be the best-case scenario.

For Lara, each of her decisions during and after her marriage put her closer or farther away from financial security. And there lies the dig. Each small decision will eventually add together to propel you to the top of the mountain, or hold you towards the bottom. The devil is truly in the details. View your financial life as a series of really important decisions that will continuously add up to create an important result. That result will incubate and take years to be birthed. But when it is, there is no turning back. Together, let's begin the journey down the road that leads to financial stability.

Money Queen Fact: Marriage eases the financial burden, but most women outlive their male partners. Two-thirds of men over 65 live with a partner, while less than half (44%) of women over 65 live with a partner.[8]

Finding Balance

While we all need to put time and money towards our own happiness, it's important to keep our finances in balance, and that means planning for the future. Remember that obtaining a positive financial position requires positive financial practices. Whether you want to start a family, save for retirement, or go on a dream vacation one day, the only way you can get there is by planning ahead. I always tell people to start planning as soon as possible—and the younger you are, the better off you'll be—simply because you have time on your side. Time is a powerful thing. Money is replaceable; time is not. You can make more money, but you cannot find more time. Time allows you to make mistakes, learn from those mistakes, and then do better the next time around. You can withstand a market crash, a financial disaster, or any other issue that would appear to be less manageable later in life. That is why most financial planners are comfortable with higher risk at a younger age. Mostly because there is a recovery time and you do not need the money for immediate use. Thus, beginning the process of saving and planning at an early age positions you to be ahead of the game. If you start late, you will find yourself playing the extremely difficult game of catch-up.

As a child, you lived in the present and took whatever money you had to buy what you wanted—and you could get away with it. And the reality is that your needs and wants were pretty reasonable. Some candy, a new basketball, and if you are really shooting for the stars, a nice bicycle. But things change as you mature and grow. Your financial responsibilities and requirements are much higher. Your wants and desires increase as well. And you may even find yourself in a position to support a family or raise children—all of which can get very expensive. So, as an adult, we cannot just turn to our parents for the little amount of money we once needed. Your mindset needs to include not just living in the *now*, but living *for* the future. Learning how to create budgets, how to balance your checkbook, and to appreciate the importance of saving money are all common and simple things that parents typically teach; however, they don't always cover bigger, more complicated topics like credit scores and investment strategies.

That's where I come in. Let's start with the basics and go from there.

---

*Money Queen Fact: 86% of women do not know
how to invest or choose a financial product.*[9]

The Credit Crunch

At the core of your financial world is a number that determines your financial trustworthiness. So just when you think you're done with studying, exams, and worrying about your grades, guess what? You now have another, much more important number to study for the rest of your life: your credit score. It is literally the backbone of everything that happens moving forward.

But what does your credit score have to do with financial planning? Well, every decision you make with your credit today can impact your ability to obtain credit tomorrow. That means you should make sure you are responsible and make timely payments if you apply for and obtain a credit card in college. It means you should pay your rent on time, ensure your cable bill and power bill are handled by their due dates, and not overspend and stretch your credit to the limits at a young age. This is not where you should try to play catch up. Thus, the credit crunch starts as early as you can obtain credit. Build your credit early, maintain responsible practices with your spending and payments, and start planning early to obtain a high credit score to ensure you are ready when you need it. Because there will be a day very soon where you will need it. Deciding to buy a house? Good credit will get you qualified. How about a car? Unless you have the money in hand, you will have to apply for a loan. What about opening a credit card? Only if you have good credit. With great credit there are endless opportunities. Without it, you will find yourself stuck. Stuck in a limited world where you cannot obtain the credit needed to build your life.

Most of us gain a rudimentary understanding of credit (an industry term for borrowing) as young adults, as it is at the heart of our economy. We learn through our parents, loved ones, and even the media. It is an oft-discussed topic and at some point in your life, your parents probably moved into a new home or purchased a new car on credit. Everyone has a credit report, which details their borrowing history and then calculates it into a single number to help potential lenders judge a borrower's credit worthiness. There are many things included in this number, but here are the essentials you should consider:

- **Payment history.** Remember that timely payments are more important than paying in full. Even if you pay the minimum every month, schedule reminders in your phone or on your computer to do so early.

- **Amounts owed.** If you add up every penny you owe, what is your overall debt? Try to strike a middle point here, having enough credit/debt to show a course of payments and positive conduct, but not so much that a credit card company would not be willing to give you the opportunity to create even more.

- **Length of credit history.** How long have you been borrowing money? The longer your history, the better. Even if you open one credit card and only charge groceries on it, demonstrating timely and consistent payments can help you increase your credit score and your ability to obtain even more credit when needed.

- **New credit.** Have you applied for any new credit recently? Credit card companies are weary of folks who apply for credit on a regular basis, especially if the reason is because you keep getting turned down.

- **Types of credit used.** Lenders like to see a variety of credit types: bank cards, car loans, student loans, etc…Apply for a credit card through your school, maybe even a gas card, and certainly make sure you are paying your own car payment, even if your parents are reimbursing you. Do the best you can do at an early age to take the small steps necessary to lay the foundation for strong credit history when it will ultimately be needed the most.

With that said, let's take a quick look at how your credit score is broken down. Credit scores can range from the low end of 300, all the way to the perfect score of 850. On average, the median score for today's adult is 700.

Excellent 750-850
Good 700-749
Fair 640-699
Poor 580-639
Very Poor 300-579

Higher credit scores improve the chances of lenders extending credit to you—whether it's a car loan, an apartment rental, a mortgage, or a business loan. Depending on your profession, especially in the financial industry, potential employers might also check your credit history to see how fiscally responsible you are. They have the right, and certainly the responsibility, to ensure that any money loaned is in fact a good investment. So rest assured that short of your blood type, they are going to work to acquire as much pertinent information as possible.

Everyone starts out with no credit. The best time to begin building your credit is while you are still in school, as it is the only time in your life that you will be able to get a credit card without a job or income. Banks like the idea of forming relationships with the general public at a younger age. So they are willing to take a chance on a young adult, offering a lower spending limit and monitoring them often to ensure they are meeting the minimum expectations. Remember that if you manage your credit card well, you can start out with good credit at a young age.

Building credit can be a vicious cycle because you can't get credit without already having credit. So, what do you do if you didn't take advantage of having a student credit card while still in school? Here are two additional ways to build your credit:

- **Take out a secured loan.** Banks will lend you a sum of money and you pay it back in monthly installments (plus interest, of course). This is very controlled and banks deem this as a low-risk investment.

- **Have a co-signer.** Have someone with an established credit history help you open a credit card. You don't need a co-signer for student credit cards. Most parents are willing to co-sign for their children's cards, reducing the stress and anxiety a lender may feel because of little, if any, outstanding credit history.

But remember, not all credit is good credit. You may have heard that opening a store credit card (*Target*, *Macy's*, etc.) is a good way to build credit. While this is true, opening them might also hurt your credit. Let me explain.

When you apply for a credit card, a lender checks your history. This is referred to as a "hard inquiry." This will appear on your credit report and the result is a decrease in your credit score. In contrast, "soft inquiries" are other inquiries in which your credit score is checked, but not by a potential lender, instead it might be something like a credit check for a rental application. These happen often and have little, if any, bearing on your overall credit score. Now, a "hard inquiry" does not have much of a lasting impact on your number, but it can create short-term concern. Often, the increase in your credit score created by building credit history is outweighed by the quick hit the "hard inquiry" causes.

Everyone should make it a priority to know their credit score. It is important to review your credit report and check your credit score at least once every year. You are entitled to one free credit check per year. That's right—by law, you can get a free copy of your credit report every twelve months from each credit reporting company. This is to ensure the information on all of your credit reports is accurate and up to date. Simply go to *annualcreditreport.com* to learn how to get your reports. Not many things in life are free, so take advantage of this opportunity! Remember, you are getting your credit report, not your credit score; you will have to pay for that. The cost isn't much, usually around $20.00 or so. It's worth that little bit to know where you stand. In addition to knowing your credit history, you can ensure there were no inaccuracies impacting your overall score. It can also protect against identity theft and ensure you are making the correct representations to potential lenders as you apply for credit in the future.

Money Queen Fact: *According to Philip Cohen, a sociologist at the University of Maryland, in the past 20 years, the glass ceiling hasn't moved much. The percentage of women managers rose only 3% (from 35% to 38%).*

Besides *annualcreditreport.com*, there are many sites from which to receive copies of your credit report. Most of them require a credit card number. Be careful of websites that promise a free report then sign you up for monthly, paid monitoring...that may create a bill you weren't ready or willing to pay. There is *LifeLock*, for example, which offers different levels of service. I subscribe and pay $19 a month. I am notified each time anyone looks at my credit report or attempts to open up an account with my social security number or personal data. It is worth the peace of mind for me. There are many sites out there offering totally free credit reports. One that I recommend to all of my clients is *CreditKarma.com*. Not only do you get your credit report, but you also get to see your credit score, which is something that is not offered by all sites. You can also continue to monitor changes as time goes on. Regardless of your website of choice, pick one and schedule an annual reminder to double check that credit score to ensure you are moving up, and not down.

Checking your score on a regular basis also allows you to check for inaccuracies and any potential identity theft. If there are any errors, it is vital that you dispute the information right away with the Credit Bureau to have it resolved. If you notice an incorrect address or account that is not yours, you will have to contact the credit bureaus individually. The three major credit bureaus in the U.S. are Equifax, Experian, and TransUnion. They each have their own ways of managing disputes, whether it is through direct phone calls, email, web, or snail mail. Also, you may discover that information will be incorrect on one report and not another. Since not all companies report to all three credit bureaus, you may find that you have slightly different credit scores from each bureau. Thus, make sure you are consistent and take the time on either an annual or bi-annual basis to confirm the validity and accuracy of your reporting.

Now that you understand how credit scores work, you can start to understand why keeping up with your finances is so important. Even a small blemish on your credit history like a missed or late payment can not only accrue interest over time, but also negatively impact your future hopes of obtaining loans or anything involving a background check of your credit. The bottom line is that your credit score is a direct result of your financial decisions, whether you like it or not.

Chapter 4

YOUR BEST FINANCIAL LIFE

Within each of us, we all have what can be deemed as "earning capacity." That is, we all have a threshold or possibility to create and earn income over the course of our careers. So much of our earning capacity can be directly attributed to our upbringing, education, work ethic, desire, determination, opportunities, and maybe even a little bit of luck along the way. Regardless of the factors at play, we each have a very special island in the middle of a beautiful ocean. That island has all we need to survive. It is paradise. Warm sun, fresh food, crystal clear water, and everything else you'd imagine in your perfect corner of the world. Sounds great, doesn't it? This is how to envision living your "*best financial life.*" It is your Utopia of financial security.

But it is not as if you will be whisked away and taken there by helicopter or plane at the push of a button. It takes time and energy to land on this perfect place. But it is entirely within your life's potential. This island is calm and comforting. It will be the culmination of all you have done throughout your life. And it will be worth every penny of the money you save and the intelligent financial decisions you make. But before we can set our feet in the sand, let's visualize how paradise may look.

Early in life, you should consider what this island looks like. Who is there? What is there? What is not there? Together, we are going to map out your perfect financial life. Let's start by defining what your *"best financial life"* really looks like. To me, someone's best financial life lies at the intersection of their available resources and their ultimate goals. Women, ready to make a plan should use their ideal future as the base, and make adjustments according to life's realities and constant changes to ensure they reach their goal in both a timely and efficient manner.

One important aspect of this concept hinges on what you *can and cannot control.* Too many times, my clients focus on those things they cannot control. In fact, they harp on them, preventing forward movement and growth. You cannot control your age or what you have done with your finances to this point. But you can quickly make changes and begin the journey down an entirely different path. With that said, we will spend the majority of our time together focusing on those things we do have control over. It's important to balance the things you can control: what you save, what you spend, what you leave and to whom you leave it when you pass away, what you have when you retire, how you choose to invest the money you earn and save, and how you plan and handle unforeseen factors such as taxes, rises and falls in the stock market, or even natural disasters like hurricanes, floods, and fires.

Generally speaking, there are five factors that each of us can control within our financial environment:

1. What we save
2. What we spend
3. When we retire
4. What we risk or don't risk
5. How much we want to leave when we pass away

Using these controls, we are able to construct a plan. One part of the master plan that I find useful is the *Financial Control Scorecard.* My firm, United Capital, uses this as a means of evaluating your position in your financial life. We also track your score over time to see how you are progressing. This is a number, similar to your credit score, which is a predictor of your potential success in meeting your goals, based on thousands of random outcomes. It helps tell us your daily financial status, based on your goals and expectations, and it enables us to make proactive tradeoffs and sacrifices to remain in line with your goals. From there, we can use it to play with your controllable factors and see how each affects the score.

These little experiments can occur at any time. For instance, last summer, a client of mine received a buy-off package from her employer. Concerned about how this would affect her future goals, we ran the numbers to see what her financial scorecard would show. Once she saw how the change affected her score in a positive way, she decided to accept the buy-off. More often than not, these financial scores often act as positive reinforcement, allowing my clients to feel at ease with their financial decisions.

Remember, many folks make financial decisions based solely on emotions. My client mentioned above could have easily felt slighted because of the offer to terminate and buy-off her contract and declined the offer. Who knows what the response would be? But after removing the emotion from the equation and quantifying the perspective decision, the facts didn't lie. It was a monumentally intelligent decision to accept the offer, remove her emotions from the decision, and move on.

But, no matter how well the "best financial life" concept works—some clients become nervous when they first hear about the scorecard. As a society, we are instilled with the notion that performance is a measurement of success, but we cannot look at the scorecard in that frame. It's simply a number that is relevant to *you* and what *you* want from *your* life; it's not about performance or getting the best grade. Ultimately, making a plan with your goals and dreams in mind is about growing your bottom line and net worth in order to gain the ability to spend however you see fit. After all, doesn't everyone deserve to live a little?

Accountability

According to the dictionary, *accountability* is defined as an obligation or willingness to accept responsibility for one's actions. It's the liability of being called to account; it's being answerable. Your best financial life begins with the notion that you have complete and utter control over both your journey and your destination. You have to be accountable for where you have been and where you plan to go. Each and every decision you make with your money will impact your opportunity to reach the very specific goals that you set forth. At the end of the day, it is your money. You earned it, you can spend it however you see fit. But once you begin to make financial decisions with accountability at the forefront of those decisions, you will find that you begin to inch closer to your desired results. But the exciting part of this is that if you believe that you are accountable for your financial future, then you can also believe that you are in complete control of it. There is no finger pointing or blame to shell out. Good or bad, it is on you. Remember a dollar earned and a dollar spent will both influence whether your financial road will be paved with gold or concrete.

Money Queen Fact: 6% is the median contribution
of women who participate in their employer's plan.[10]

Accountability plays an important role in all aspects of your life. From finishing those pesky reports at work, to paying the bills at home and even taking care of the family pet, your daily tasks all require a certain level of responsibility and carry certain consequences. If you do not accomplish a specific goal, or even fall short, there is only one person at which you can point fingers.

What happens when you can't see the consequences? What happens when you start living in the now, and not living for the future? Well in the world of financial planning, that's where accountability comes in. Accountability is the guiding light as you navigate this obstacle-ridden journey. It keeps you focused, aware, and responsible for those steps you do take and those that you don't.

Whether it's for retirement, college tuition, or to purchase their dream house, as a Financial Planner, it's my goal to help all of my clients reach their financial goals. Getting there is the hard part. But accountability makes it easier. It makes the waters calmer and easier to cross.

Although I may not see my clients very often—sometimes only once a year—I still like to keep them on track and working towards a future goal. It is important to ensure they are constantly being held accountable to our plan and their goals. And there lies much of the value with a financial planner. Accountability is a team game. Look at yourself like the star player. When it comes down to it, you are running up and down the court and ultimately doing the hard work. But it is very helpful to have an experienced coach that can help you take a few steps back and look at the whole game without getting lost in the unimportant details or emotions involved.

The same is true in financial planning. As planners, we have a wealth of knowledge to impart on our clients. But we also help to communicate and convey the additional skills required to be intelligent and informed savers and spenders. We also hold our clients accountable through helping them not only make important decisions with their money, but also reflect on the missteps and the frivolous spending, when it occurs.

It's very important to check in with my clients, regardless of how often we meet. Sometimes my clients need a little reminder that, no matter when they come to see me, they should always be working towards that one goal.

Most of the time I try to keep my clients on the right track, but I can only guide them so far. When it comes down to it, clients need to hold themselves accountable for their actions. The money is gone once it is spent. We cannot get it back. But habits are formed over time and through making the same decision again and again. The goal is to ensure that these habit-forming behaviors are positive and beneficial ones. Clients who have a long-term vision and who are self-disciplined have an easier time with this, as it's in their nature.

Money Queen Fact: 57% of women say a fear of running out of money keeps them up a night.[11]

Those individuals who are not wired this way may need a little extra help. If this is you, here are a few suggestions to try in your daily life that might help keep you on track toward reaching your goals through accountable practices:

- Make a list. This will help to keep you organized through the process; and let's be honest, there's always some gratification in crossing a line off of a to-do list.
- Share your goals with your family and friends. Those people in your daily life can provide positive reinforcement as well as hold you to high standards across the board.

- Go public! Social media provides numerous platforms on which you can update your followers about your progress. It also helps to do this on a regular basis, as it keeps you accountable since you wouldn't want to let others down.
- Keep your goal(s) posted in a place where you can see them. The constant reminder helps keep it in the front of your mind. Pick a private place in your office or home where you constantly chart your financial progress to ensure you are making the decisions to reach your goals.

It's always important to remember that anything worth having takes time, so patience is a must. As long as you continue to hold yourself accountable, your goals are obtainable—financial or otherwise.

Changes

Remember when you were younger? You didn't think much about saving money. Heck, you probably didn't think much about spending it either. Money came and money went. At the end of the day, it didn't matter much. Your responsibilities were few and far in between and many of us had the safety net of our parents to catch us if we fell. But times change. As you mature and age, you will quickly find that money has more value and meaning. As you leave the protective shelter of your parent's home, you will seemingly become more self-sufficient and reliant on your own ability to provide for yourself and for those you love. You will also view money in a different light as you work enormously hard to earn it.

It's funny how attitudes change, as you get older. When you were a kid, you couldn't wait to be an adult—getting to live by your own rules, celebrating your own independence, and finding your own way. It sounded amazing, right? But as you mature, your outlook shifts. You start to yearn for those younger years when parents and teachers dictated life decisions, and the only things you really worried about were homework, crushes, and what to do on the weekend. For all intents and purposes, it really was a lot easier then.

Unfortunately for us, time travel doesn't exist. We can't go back to simpler times to escape the troubles of adulthood. Change is a natural part of life. And your financial situation will change time and time again as you grow. So we must embrace these changes and new founded responsibilities. And the sooner the better. Whether you're fresh out of school, gaining your footing in your professional life, or embarking on a new personal adventure, responsibilities will always be building, changing, and evolving. And that is very exciting and should be celebrated.

Every phase of your life is filled with great personal change…it's tough at times, but it's how we grow. There are always new things to experience: careers to start, trips to take, and new relationships to form. Plus, every woman's story is different and unique—some of us will find jobs that we love and stay at the same company for years. Others will move around before finding the perfect spot, while there is still a group of us that will opt to go at it alone, starting our own businesses. Regardless of the path we each take, financial gain, loss, and hopefully saving will play a pivotal role in your journey. It is simply a natural part of our personal and professional lives. The school of thought this book prescribes to is one centered on the notion that starting young is the best way to obtain financial security and comfort. It gives you more flexibility, safety, and opportunity. That means that you should start saving, or at least have a plan for saving in place, as soon as your college years. That doesn't mean you shouldn't spend money or enjoy life. What it does mean is that you should always be responsible, cognizant, and accountable towards your money. And the sooner the better.

The remainder of the book will start with your college years and take you through retirement. It will focus on the responsibilities and the likely scenarios you will face during each decade of your life. Together, we will educate you and offer you information so you will be better prepared for what lies ahead. Knowledge isn't just power, it can also be money. It can result in enormous earning and savings potential and position you and your loved ones for great success. But, if nothing else, it will certainly reduce much of the stress that most women feel in regards to their financial situations. And the less stress we have in our lives, the more readily available we will be to enjoy it.

Throughout this book, we will discuss the steps you can take now to create financial stability later in life. Unless you win the lottery, it literally takes a lifetime to build and maintain financial comfort. And that is assuming you start on time. Unfortunately, most people don't. But that doesn't mean that you cannot make the changes now to impact your life later. Remember, it starts with accountability. Be accountable for the decisions you have made and those you will inevitably make. Sometimes the hardest part is deciding to change your financial tendencies. But I am confident with the tools and resources in place, you won't fall into the trap that so many before you have. We can build financial security. And we can change bad habits and poor practices. We can do it together, I promise!.

Chapter 5

YOUR ROARING 20's:
THE JOURNEY BEGINS

Now that the backdrop has been set, we can start to navigate your ideal financial life. Start at an early age. I cannot say it enough. I could scream it to the mountains. It is the simplest yet most powerful financial advice I can offer you. It opens the doors of options for you and your life. The sooner you begin to save, the better position you will be in to succeed in saving. Start early, stay focused, and constantly reflect and analyze your journey.

Your 20's are a time for growth, discovery, and exploration both personally and professionally. You will begin the process of growing and maturing in preparation for beginning your career. In your, you will receive valuable training and education that will probably be the foundation for the rest of your life. For many, they can be a roaring good time. It is the start of the journey of both life and financial security. This is where the foundation for the castle is built. In some form, most women want independence. It's a huge part of a happy life. Independence in love, in life, and in finances are all coveted and sought after in your twenties. The trouble is few of us take the time to realize and define what being independent means in our own lives. Independence often sneaks up on us. It comes fast once your education is finished and keeps popping up again and again later in life as you make choices like starting a business, moving to a new home in a new city, or even after a divorce. Independence means you're on your own, and that can be simultaneously exhilarating and terrifying. But it is a necessary and important part of life.

Managing money is usually a component of fear, and part of the reason for that fear is that the basics of building a budget are something too few of us learned right out of the gate. It's a major contributing reason to why money makes smart women feel dumb. In grade school we learn math, and in college we are often taught the fundamentals of business and economics, but rarely are we taught in a scholastic setting how to create a financially successful life. Those lessons are usually reserved for a trial by fire approach. But they do not have to be. Just like you learn your core curriculum in college, financial planning should be part of your core curriculum in life.

But the good news is you can create a workable budget at any age with a little bit of information. There are a few simple steps anyone can take to create a manageable financial life that leaves room for saving not just for the future, but also for living a little in the present. Step one is to take stock of where you are in life right now, and maybe make some decisions about changes that might be made. In your twenties, life should be financially relative; responsibilities are low, but so are your earnings.

Start with your work life to begin the process of evaluating your financial scenario. Since the product of your work life is how you'll pay your bills, take a look at it to determine exactly what is going on. Are you working part-time or full-time? Are you actively seeking different employment?

Even if you're not clocking in 40 hours, you can take a small amount out to contribute to a 401(k) or another savings plan. As a college student, you may have a part time or weekend job. It may supplement your student loans, or even what your parents give you. But no matter what, you should agree to put a small portion of those earnings aside for savings.

---

*Money Queen Fact: 61% of women are
offered a 401(k) or similar plan.*[12]

When you have completed college and entered the real world, it is even more important to consider savings. Think in terms of taking baby steps. If you're making $30,000 a year, for instance, you can start by contributing 3% each week. This is a percentage that is probably small enough that it won't cause any hardship. You probably wont even know it is gone. Here's a sample equation of what an annual 401(k) contribution might look like, plus a subtraction for taxes, to get a clearer view of your monthly take home income:

$30,000
- $900   401(k) contribution
$29,100   taxable income
- $5,820   Taxes
= $23,280   Divided by 12 = $1,940 a month to live on

As you can see, it is imperative to start with your savings. It is the crux of your future financial success. Next, think about what's making up your recurring expenses and reducing your ability to save more. Where do you live? Are you on your own or do you live with a partner or roommate, or with your parents? Each scenario has different pros, cons, and financial implications, and your living situation is likely to be the biggest concern when it comes to balancing your finances. It will probably encompass your biggest monthly expense. But it can be controlled and should certainly be budgeted for as an initial step.

Rent, or a mortgage, is the largest bill in the stack. And it is the one that comes every month without fail. In fact, it's one reason why the number of adults moving home to live with their parents is on the rise. Eliminating that bill allows young men and women to forego a large expense and begin the process of aggressively saving for a future home. According to a recent Pew Research Center study, 36% of adults ages 18 to 31 are opting to live at home these days, and for many it's a wise choice.

Finally, what's your lifestyle like? Do you have hefty car payments, a tendency to go out with friends every weekend, or a hobby that takes a piece of your financial pie each month? Perhaps you have a pet that not only needs to eat and play, but visit the vet on a regular basis. These are all parts of the mix. Rent or mortgage is like a big train headed down the tracks. These other bills are more like a traffic-jam. They are smaller, but certainly can add up to impact your financial situation. In fact, these are usually where you can cut the most. Take the time to assess where your money goes each month to consider where you can save more. You may find out you eat out ten times per week and spend over $300.00 on food at restaurants. You may be able to reduce these outings and save $100/month or $1200/year. These small victories inevitably add up over time.

Next, take the time to add up all of your current bills. When you are on your own, you're 100% responsible for your financial life, so your budget becomes a chart of what parts make up the whole. From this point, you can make adjustments to create a balance, and some changes may be larger than others. Keep in mind that the ultimate goal is creating a financial picture that makes sense both now and for the coming years. One that doesn't have you holed up in one room every day, afraid to even turn on an extra light, let alone go out for dinner once in a while. You may decide it makes sense to move home with your parents, or even find a friend with which to rent an apartment. It is an act of balancing your goals and desires against your current financial situation.

For instance, think about your commute. Do you own or make payments on a car? Do you need to buy a car, or do you live in an area where mass transit is an option? In addition to the car itself, factor in the costs of insurance, gas, and regular maintenance. Look for the best deals on all of the above, especially car insurance. If you're under 25, you may be able to stay on your parent's insurance and can then pay them directly. Some companies offer discounts if you don't drive often or for long distances, if you have a safe driving record, or if you pay half of the premium up front. Be a smart consumer and price check with multiple providers before you make the best decision for your situation. And remember that you shouldn't always purchase the least expensive insurance. Make sure you are well protected because spending a little more on the frontend can save you an enormous amount of money on the backend if disaster strikes. Do some homework to find the least expensive option for your needs, and remember that regulations differ from state-to-state.

You can approach health insurance in much the same way—there are several options to explore. Discern what's going to work best for you. Is it the *Affordable Care Act*? Is there affordable insurance offered through your workplace? Have you recently lost benefits? In the latter case, you may find you are eligible for COBRA. Depending on your age and circumstances, health insurance is another area where your parents might be able to help by adding you to their policy.

And the list goes on and on. Keep running down your list of expenses. Chances are utilities, such as heat or electricity, food, and your cell phone aren't far behind home, car, and health—followed by any number of miscellaneous and 'entertainment' expenses. Cable television can take out quite a chunk of your monthly budget, for example. Today, however, there are countless options to shrink this at-home expense. Services such as *Netflix* or *Hulu* can offer television shows and movies for less than ten dollars a month, and there are Internet options that take terrestrial television out of the equation completely, relying solely on internet-based signals. The point is that the options are endless. One thing we have in this country is enormous choice. Prioritize what is most important for you and then do your best to reduce and cut the rest. There are plenty of small steps you can take now to save money for your future.

There are always going to be expenses, but there are many ways to save a dollar, too. The big takeaway is to be responsible, consistently check the pulse of your financial life, and also be creative and think outside of the box with your financial decisions. Find out how much things really cost, look for deals, and as Matthew McConaughey said in the iconic coming-of-age film *Dazed and Confused*, "Keep on livin'."

Money for Nothing

The notion of money for nothing sounds like an exciting one, right? Well rest assured that there is no such thing as "free" money. Borrowing money always comes at a cost, both personally and financially. And in your twenties, you will be faced with making one of your biggest initial financial decisions. It can have a lasting effect on your credit score and can impact your financial journey for years to come. You guessed it—student loans. For many of us, it was the first major financial decision we ever made, around the age of 18, when we were very new to the notion of financial responsibility.

Money Queen Fact: *In an analysis of census data by*
Reach Advisors, a market research firm, in the majority of
U.S. cities, single women ages 22 to 30 without children
have a higher median income than their male peers.

Sometimes, it feels as if everyone has student loan debt. The problem with this is that's how today's students, who are about to enter college, see it as well. *If everyone comes out of school with debt,* they think, *why would I choose a school with my future finances in mind?*

Here's why they should: A student with a $20,000 loan (the national average is $25,000) with a 5% fixed interest rate, paid back over 10 years, will be responsible for a $377 payment each month. With at least four years between the student and her first bill, those numbers are blurry at best, but applied to real-life purchases, they begin to come into focus. For some, it's a car payment on a Lexus, or for others, a rent check.

Whatever puts that figure into real terms for someone—a new couch, a weekend getaway, and the ability to start a business—then that's it. The reality is that it is money taken right out of your pocket each and every month. In these early years, students should definitely consider the academic programs, location, and student body of a college. But they also need to ask questions like, "What's the interest rate on my loans going to be?" Right now, many, if not most, simply don't. Going to your dream school might make you happy at the time, but later on, the looming burden of student loans can affect your chances at securing a mortgage, a line of credit, or achieving financial independence in general.

Now, I am not telling you to forego a great educational opportunity because it costs a little more than that safety school to which you were accepted. What I am offering is the notion that you should consider the real life cost of all your financial decisions and weigh those before making any decisions. Remember to take your emotions out of it, and clearly evaluate what things cost before you act. Then, feel free to put on that college sweatshirt and wave the flag while singing your new fight song.

Managing Your Student Loans

In your twenties, there is a high likelihood you will spend time filling out applications for student loans. Most of us realize the value in a college degree, but we also recognize the enormous financial commitment required to obtain a collegiate diploma. And it can get even worse if you decide to enter into a graduate degree program. You want to become a doctor or a lawyer, you say? The financial commitment will be simply remarkable. Borrowing money in any capacity can feel extremely stressful and scary, especially if you are not familiar with the rules of the game.

I can remember the conversation like it occurred yesterday. Years ago, my father kindly informed me he would pay for 100% of the costs associated with an education at a state school, or he said I could attend a private school of my own choosing and take out loans for the difference. Like most college-bound students, I was 18, and had no clue what I to do. After a long conversation with my father, I quickly determined taking on debt would be a horrendous and unnecessary decision. So off to the State University of New York I went. I was one of the lucky ones.

Money Queen Fact: Women today earn the majority of doctorates and master's degrees, and nearly 60% of U.S. college students are women.[13]

But now, more than ever, a large amount of young adults recognize the value in a higher education, and face the harsh realization it will be on their own dime. They don't have the money now, so they have no choice but to borrow it and pay it back later. The difficult learning experience I avoided with student loans was quickly evident by watching everyone else. Many of my friends and loved ones have fought a difficult battle with paying back their loans.

The day those checks arrived was better than Christmas. The bars and restaurants were packed. I even remember guys going out and buying new wardrobes. I was secretly jealous. Where was my windfall of free money? Why didn't I apply for these pennies from heaven? Well, the truth is that all good things come to an end and the debts eventually had to be satisfied. If we only knew then what we know now: Irresponsible spending and creating large debt early in life is a financial death sentence. So, together we will discuss the different options available and how to minimize the risk of borrowing thousands and thousands of dollars.

Choosing the Right Loan for You

There are numerous types of loans available to college-bound students. But, the first step is applying to schools you are willing to pay for. Consider the amount of money you are willing to borrow and research the tuition of each school to which you are applying. Ensure they are within your financial budget and that you are comfortable with the overall price tag.

Additionally, consider other potential expenses like the cost of living, food, books, and other incidentals like travel and the need for a vehicle. Depending on the location of the school, there may be astronomical requirements you should consider. Take the time to sit down and create a spreadsheet outlining all of your potential costs for each semester. That will give you an opportunity to truly understand how much this may cost in the long run.

Next, familiarize yourself with the available loan options available. To offer a global perspective of the most popular choices, consider the following:

Stafford Loans. Stafford Loans are the most common type of loans. They are federal education loans. Based on income, they can be either subsidized or unsubsidized. A subsidized loan is one where the government pays the interest while the student is in college. Once the student graduates, the balance of their loan is only principle and carries no required interest to be satisfied. Unsubsidized loans accrue interest while the student is in college and the student must repay interest and principal.

Perkins Loans. Perkins Loans are very low interest (currently at 5%) federal loans and are based on income. Only those students who show exceptional financial need can qualify and apply for these types of loans.

PLUS Loans. PLUS Loans are loans that can cover the "other expenses" that aren't covered by Stafford or Perkins loans, such as books and supplies. The benefit to these is that it offers you the opportunity to subsidize other fixed costs you will experience during your educational journey.

Institutional Loans. Institutional loans are loans that are given to students by the institutions they attend. They are not affiliated with the government and are much less common than federal loans.

Private Loans. Private loans are loans that are not funded by the government, but generally made by a bank or other lending institution. They have a variety of different terms, interest rates, etc. They are not fixed and can often be negotiated with the lending institution. Students who do not meet the financial need criteria for federal loans, but still need to borrow money for their educational journey, typically obtain these loans.

There are both advantages and disadvantages to each of these loan options. Some call for specific qualification requirements while others carry specific terms that may or may not fit your financial lifestyle.

The most important thing is to ensure you are fully informed and research each option before you make a decision on which loan is right for you.

What's the Debt?

When applying for college, students should first try to obtain any "free" money that they can get. Since most loan programs are capped at a certain amount per year, additional options like scholarships, work-study programs, and federal grants should always be at the top of the list before applying for any type of loan. For example, students obtaining subsidized Stafford Loans are capped at $3,500 in year 1, $4,500 in year 2 and $5,500 in years 3+, with a maximum of $23,000 borrowed over the course of the loan. Thus, there may be a gap between what you borrow and what you need. There are numerous programs and websites that offer very detailed and thorough information regarding the available loan options, and many even allow you to enter your information and your needs and will suggest the right loan option for you.

For any federal loans, students apply via their college application. Students can apply for the maximum amount, compare the loan terms and then accept only what they need. Many students choose to accept the maximum amount they can get and live off of the funds that they don't need for tuition. However, in many cases, interest is accruing on these funds so it may be a very nearsighted approach to managing your money.

The point is that you have to understand the overall exposure to your life and your finances. Everything may seem up and up in the beginning, but understand that these loans will eventually mature and you will be on the hook for every dollar you borrowed. Before applying for any loan, the most important step to take is to research and understand your exposure, including principal and interest, so you can budget accordingly.

Too Late...What Now?

Many students reading this book have already applied for and received student loans. But rest assured, there are steps you can take under your current loan structure to minimize the financial strain they may cause later in life. As previously noted, students don't have to accept all of the funds. Meeting with the financial aid department of your respective college will enable you to decline a portion of the financial aid if you choose to do so. Unfortunately, the amount of financial aid offered by the federal government is allocated among students pretty quickly and if students wait too long, the only option for obtaining additional financial assistance is through private loans (which will likely require a co-signer as many college students don't' have credit at such a young age).

Furthermore, remember that there is always a continuing opportunity to apply for scholarships and grants. Hundreds of thousands of dollars in scholarships are lost each year because students simply don't apply. There are many different types of scholarships available. The first place to start is your respective college's student handbook publication. These handbooks will generally list all scholarships available at the university. In fact, many alumni create scholarships in honor or in memory of someone. Some scholarships are available to all students while others are focused on a particular degree of study. Also, community organizations and companies offer scholarships, and while these aren't as common, a little research could go a long way.

The point is that your loans are a living and breathing organism. There is always an opportunity to restructure or lessen the blow by subsidizing your costs through grants and scholarships. A little paper work could be the difference of thousands of dollars in forgiven debt.

Always consider the occasion to repay your loans. If you are currently in the middle of your college career and are already receiving loans for your education, start paying them back now. A summer or weekend job could create enough financial opportunity to pay down your loans or even borrow a lower amount. Remember, the less you borrow, the less you will owe. The less you owe, the less interest you'll have to pay once you conclude your education. A hundred dollars here and a hundred dollars there over the course of your lengthy education could make a substantial difference in the pinch your loans may create once they mature.

Graduation

We all think about graduation day as one of the happiest times of our lives. But it is also the first day of the rest of your life. Soon, you will be on your own, ineligible for further loans, and positioned to get a job and begin the process of paying back what you owe. Loans backed by the federal government generally carry a six-month deferment period after a student graduates. This gives students a little time to find a job and get on their feet before requiring them to begin repayment. During this time, students should work to consolidate their loans. Not only will it make life simpler, but also student loan repayments are often based on the new graduate's income.

For example, if a student graduates and owes $20,000 at a 6.8% interest rate (the current Stafford Loan rate) and the standard 10-year amortization, the payment would be about $230 per month. If the student is only earning $30,000 annually, then the student loan payment as a percentage of income is almost 10%. Most of the time, programs will work with the graduates to reduce the payment in the short term and increase it when earnings increase. Additionally, you can defer payment if you continue for an advanced degree.

Money Queen Fact: Women working full time earn 81 cents on the dollar as compared to their male peers working full time.[14]

Thus, the first step for any new graduate is consolidation. Once the loans are consolidated and the graduate has worked with the lender to get a reasonable payment relative to their income, then we use the same repayment principles that we always use (in most cases, high interest debt is knocked out first and then lower interest debt is paid). The good news is that most interest on your student loans is tax deductible and can be written off. But you still have to budget. I have worked with clients who are locked in at extremely high rates while the current loan rate is half of what they are paying. It is difficult for them to watch loan rates decrease and their high interest rate remain the same. One particular client had major trouble paying back her loans at a high rate and it followed her for over 15 years. So much so that she was denied a mortgage because of missed payments and her debt to income ratio.

The point is that a bad decision in your twenties (or even earlier) can follow you for the better part of your adult years. It is easy to fall into the attitude that you can deal with this later in life, but eventually later will become now. And then you are stuck. So, make informed and financially intelligent decisions early in the process to ensure you are positioned to handle the debt once it comes due.

The Three Do's...
With an overview of the student loan process in mind, consider the three big do's of managing your student loans...

DO... APPLY FOR FREE MONEY. Too much scholarship money goes untouched every year. Fill out the applications, write the essays, and then submit them. The financial benefit over the longer term is tremendous.

DO... GET A PART-TIME JOB. This will not only help you reduce the amount of financial assistance you will need, but it will also show potential future employers that you've been in the work force and you can juggle many financial responsibilities. It may be the difference between getting a better job, or qualifying for a car or house loan.

DO... CONSIDER JOB OFFERS THAT FORGIVE OR REPAY STUDENT LOANS. There are numerous government positions that offer loan forgiveness or are willing to help repay a portion of your outstanding loans. The same is true in the medical industry. Salary should be just one consideration when accepting a job. Consider the total amount of money saved and earned with any potential job offer.

The Three Don'ts...

Sometimes what you don't do is just as important as what you do. Consider these important landmines you should avoid when dealing with student loans during and after college.

DO NOT... FAIL YOUR CLASSES. If you do, you'll be stuck with no degree, student loan balances, and no way to go back to college as you will not be eligible to receive financial assistance if your grades don't reflect serious effort. This is the worst position you can find yourself in. You will have nothing to show for your efforts but a debt to repay.

DO NOT... ACCEPT ALL FINANCIAL ASSISTANCE IF YOU DON'T NEED IT. Doing so will cause your repayment amounts to be higher and cause you to pay back more interest than necessary. If you do not need the money, don't apply for it. Only apply and accept what you know you have to have. Ever heard the statement, "starving college student?" Don't starve yourself, but don't feast either.

DO NOT... APPLY TO ANY SCHOOL WITHOUT UNDERSTANDING THE REAL COST. Not all colleges are created equal. Some are more expensive, are located in areas that cost more to live in, and require more of you financially. Understand the whole package. Then, consider if it is worth it to you. You should never go into the process blind and feel caught off guard when that first bill comes in the mail.

Remember to educate yourself and make the best decision for you and your life.

Student loan debt never goes away—not even in bankruptcy. If you borrow the money, you will have to eventually repay it in one fashion or another. Don't want to repay it? Well, that could cost you good credit and the ability to ever take a loan out again. So, take the time to consider all of your options as well as the potential earning capacity you may have after college. Then, you can truly assess the right type of loan for you. Next, assess how much you truly will need and try not to apply for a loan over that amount. The temptation of having the money may help justify the spending of it. Making intelligent and calculated decisions before you apply for your loan will minimize the impact these loans can have on you as you enter the real world.

Youthful Investing

Investing isn't something young adult's think of when they join the "real world." These days they are more concerned with student loan debt and simply getting a job in their desired field, which is often easier said than done. I am constantly asked when is the best time to start investing. My answer is always: *As soon as possible!*

You see, the time value of money is very powerful thing; I consider it the eighth wonder of the world. The more time goes on, the quicker your small investments can grow into a large nest egg. Unfortunately, most people catch on to this late in life and always say, "I wish I would have started when I was younger."

As we all know, it can be very difficult convincing a teenager or young twenty-something to delay gratification now for a greater pay off in the future. However, they tend to change their minds if you show them with real numbers.

Take this example: A young lady received $400,000 from an insurance death benefit when she was just 21 years old. By the time she even thought about doing something productive with the money, she had already spent $200,000 of it.

Do you know how much that $200,000 would be worth at 65? $350,000? Nope, not even close. If she'd invested it, with a 7.5% return, she would have increased her egg to 4.8 *million* dollars. That's what 44 years of compounding will get you because the more time you have, the more you can make. But keep in mind that this works only if you don't make decisions out of fear or greed. In other words, don't let your emotions get in the way.

Your first job is a perfect to start. If your company offers a 401(k), join it so they match whatever amount you want to set aside from each check. If they don't have one, set up an automatic investment plan on your own by saving a certain amount from your paycheck each payday. If you decide to go this route, make the deductions automatic because it's easier if it's on autopilot. So with that in mind, let's chat a little bit about obtaining that first opportunity in the real world.

Money Queen Fact: Despite longer expected life spans, when asked how much they were aiming for in retirement savings, women aimed lower with a median goal of $200,000 versus $400,000 for men.[15]

Working 9 to 5

Most of us work to support our families, to enjoy the various opportunities life offers, to purchase anything and everything, to save and prepare for life's challenges, and inevitably, for retirement. We work to get paid and we get paid to thrive as a consumer, in one manner or another. Generally speaking, the harder you work, the more money you have the occasion to make. And the more money you make, the more money you can save, assuming you aren't spending it all. All of the planning and monitoring in the world won't do a heap of good without a steady income stream coming in the door. For the majority of us, the bulk of that income is the money we generate from our chosen career.

It seems as if good jobs are harder to come by these days—just ask any recent college graduate. It used to be easier to obtain meaningful employment, but now there are so many qualified people applying for so few desirable jobs that the competition is the highest it has ever been. Most grads leave school with the idea that they'll immediately land their dream job. Unfortunately, that's rarely the case. But it doesn't mean you shouldn't try to find the perfect fit. Just know that most new entries into the workforce are finding that the journey to the peak of the mountain takes time, effort, and sometimes, more than one job. With the average job-hunt spanning at least a few months, many women quickly become eager to take whatever job offer they can get their hands on. In turn, they may end up accepting an offered salary without negotiation and little benefits—if they're lucky enough to find an employer who offers them any in the first place. Extending your search for a few months longer could prevent constant movement or the persistent urge to "look around" at other opportunities.

As soon as you get a job offer, it is important not to accept it immediately. Instead, use this time to negotiate your salary. If they want you, the simple act of asking if there is more money available, or negotiation a better set of benefits won't deter them. You may not get exactly what you wanted, but at least you asked. Remember, benefits are just as important as your salary. It is literally money in your pocket if your potential employer is willing to pick up the bill for health insurance, or your cell phone, or maybe even a car payment if you travel for work. Someone has to pay for these life necessities, so it might as well be your new employer.

This is a key part of owning your financial independence, and ruling your life as the "Queen of your Domain." Be professional and courteous, but be strong and steadfast. If you accept the position before this phase, you lose the chance to initially increase your pay and then exponentially grow it. The higher you start, the quicker you will rise. It's a good idea to have a number in mind, with the minimum being at least your cost of living. The best thing you can do is to max out what they might offer you.

A good tactic is to rely on the advertised salary range, if there is one. Say the advertised salary was $50,000-$60,000, and they offered you $45,000. You can easily ask for $5,000 more, as your offer was beneath what they originally advertised. If your potential employer won't budge, see if they offer a signing bonus. If they don't, at least take the time to assess and inquire as to why you are being offered less than the advertised number. There may be a perfectly logical explanation for this behavior, but then again, that explanation may just be that they are not a "do what they say" type of company. That is a better lesson to learn before accepting the job.

Remember, as awkward as salary negotiations can be, they are commonplace and crucial to success. Most employers are actually expecting you to counter their offer, so you may as well ask for a respectable amount more. After all, the worst thing they can say is "no."

Once you've settled on how much you'll be making each year, it's time to inquire about your benefits package. Unfortunately, benefit packages have dwindled over the years, but the average benefit package consists of insurance—usually some combination of medical, dental, and life—paid vacation and time off, 401(k) options, disability, and flexible savings, just to name a few. There are plenty of other options and it is best to inquire as to the industry standard before you meet with your potential employer so you can negotiate from a point of knowledge and information.

Money Queen Fact: Because of maternity and family leaves, which total about 13 years, retired women will receive about half the pension benefits retired men will receive.[16]

Keep in mind that not all employers offer all of these options, and some may even offer more. But it is important to take your time, read through all of the information in front of you, and then digest it all before making a decision. What benefits you decide to take advantage of is completely up to you, but if your employer offers a 401(k) and matches anything whatsoever, you need to match that minimum; otherwise, you're literally giving money away.

Some 401(k) rules of thumb: If you start early in your 20s or early 30s, put 3%-5% of your paycheck towards your 401(k). If your company matches it, you could potentially have a six-figure nest egg in as little as ten years. Remember, the sooner you begin to save, the more you will have later.

Now, when it comes to life insurance, many people don't realize the first $50,000 of life insurance is tax-free on a group policy. Knowing that, why wouldn't you consider making this small investment? However, when you're younger, you are more likely to need disability insurance rather than life insurance, so looking into the disability program is also important, especially if you're a woman thinking about having children. In some companies, pregnancy leave is part of disability insurance, not health insurance. The point is that you should read the manuals, familiarize yourself with company policies, and ensure they are consistent with your non-negotiables and expectations. Some other potential benefits you should be considering as you seek employment are:

- **Health insurance.** This is a big one to think about. HMO vs. PPO? Is there a deductible? Are there different plans? Out-of-Pocket Maximum? Consider all the options.

- **Employee Assistance Programs (EAPs).** Not everyone offers these, but EAPs can offer benefits, such as free counseling services, childcare, and training programs, to name a few.
- **Tuition Reimbursement.** Thinking about getting your MBA? Your employer may help pay for it.
- **Flexible Savings Account.** This will help pay for insurance deductibles and out-of-pocket expenses.

Is your head spinning yet? Don't worry—all of this information can be a lot to process. I would recommend talking to a friend, family member, or even a financial advisor you trust with substantial career experience to help you navigate the negotiations. It helps to have some experience on your side as you move through the confusing (yet equally exciting) world of employee benefits.

Finally, let's face it, this won't be your last negotiation. Most people have numerous jobs during their careers, so consider each negotiation as a practice session for later jobs. You'll be happy to know that over the course of your career, negotiating will become much easier. As you experience the process again and again and gain a better understanding of industry practices and norms, you will find clarity and be better positioned to prioritize what's important to you. Not only will you become more comfortable in asking for what you deserve, you can also be confident in knowing that negotiating certain benefits will have a positive impact on your financial goals.

Money Queen Fact: Only 8% of women strongly agree that they are building a large enough retirement nest egg with which to comfortably retire.

Why Should You Invest?

Now that you are hired and ready to start your earning career, let's take some time to stress the importance of setting aside some portion of your earnings each and every month.

I constantly hear women say that they are afraid of investing and would rather keep their money in the bank because it's "safe." While the bank is a great place for your checking account and emergency fund savings (three to six months of living expenses is recommended), it isn't the best place to house your money over the long-term. For purposes of our conversation, long-term investing is any amount of time greater than a five-year period. On the other hand, if you have a specific goal for which you're saving, like buying a house in ten years, you can keep it in other investment opportunities like CDs. The point is that you should always choose the investment strategy that matches your spending goals. Once you can pinpoint your immediate goals and those that will occur farther down the road, you can easily choose the best avenue to achieve those goals while still earning a return on your investment.

Most people will tell you inflation is the biggest reason *not* to keep long-term money in the bank. If your money is in the bank, it may be safe, but it is *not* keeping pace with inflation, which is currently at 3%-4%. So, your dollar is being devalued with every passing day if it is not at least earning at the rate of inflation.

Say, for instance, that you put $100,000 in the bank and earn .025% interest, which equates to $250 per year. But during that time you are losing 3% in purchasing power. In this scenario, you would actually lose $3,000 a year, making your net amount $97,250 each year. Calculate that over the course of ten years and you are losing a sizable chunk of your initial investment.

Unfortunately, this gets worse over time. In my teaching days, I would have my students (who were all in college) do an assignment where they would ask the oldest member of their family how much certain items (such as milk, a car, a house, etc.) cost when that person was young. We all joke about the relative that always says, "I remember when I was your age…" But the truth of the matter is that the valuable lesson to be learned from those memories is that inflation has accelerated the price of nearly everything we purchase as consumers. From something as small as a carton of milk or eggs to something as large as a house or car, prices have risen hundreds of thousands of percentage points.

In our exercise, my students would bring their results back and we would compare the old costs with the current ones. The results? Things that used to cost just a few cents or dollars are now much more expensive, which is a direct result of inflation. So understand that to make money over time, you have to outperform inflation. Many people are fearful that they will actually lose money by investing, but the truth is that making no decision can be as detrimental as making the wrong one.

What If?

Let's take the time to acknowledge and discuss your very real and natural fears. It is common to think, "What if I am afraid of losing all my money?" This is something I always hear as a financial planner. People even say, "Well, my friend lost *all* of their money in the stock market." My response to these people? "I am not sure if that's even possible!" But for the sake of argument, here is what I do know about losing all of your money:

- **You could loose all your money if you invested it in a Ponzi scheme.** The Maddoff investment scandal is a good example.
- **You could also lose all your money if you put all your money into *one* stock and it goes bankrupt.** But we will spend time discussing the concept of diversification later.

In the first scenario, the odds are very unlikely, and I frankly don't know why anyone would do that. In the second situation, I don't know of any diversified mutual fund that has ever gone under. Will it periodically lose money? It can. Will it rise and fall along with the market? You betcha. Will you make money if you hold it for more than ten years? Of course! Absolutely. And that is because most mutual funds mirror the market.

Money Queen Fact: *55% of women are saving for retirement outside of work in an IRA, mutual fund, bank account, etc.*[17]

Thankfully, there has never been a ten-year losing timeframe for the stock market. But rest assured, the longer the time frame and your ability to park your investment, the better it is.

So, when people ask me when they should start investing, my short and sweet answer is *absolutely, positively, right now*! After all, no one wants to run out of money or have to work forever. So the sooner you try to keep your money in sync with inflation, the better off you'll be.

Receiving an Inheritance

While most of us dream about coming into money, for a lucky few, that becomes a reality. Welcome to the world of inheritance, where money and property is passed along after the death of a loved one. Emotional times like these may not be the best in which to deal with finances, but sometimes you just can't escape the inevitable immediacy of such events.

Receiving and managing an inheritance can be stressful, especially for the younger generation who has never before had money. Most "twenty-somethings" are making smaller salaries than their older counterparts, and simply don't have the financial experience to manage their newfound and very immediate wealth. Thus, when they come into money, the experience can be an unbelievably unique and overwhelming journey to navigate.

During the course of my career, I lost count of how many times young women lose loved ones and inherit a large sum of money and don't know what to do with it, simply from lack of experience. Friends and family come out of the woodwork, and because some people feel guilty for having the money and receiving so much of it at one time, they end up giving much of it away.

Even if you think you're giving away money for a good reason, keep in mind that you could have made that money work for you, and for those you love. Imagine if you received a $400,000 inheritance in your early twenties and gave away $150,000 of it to friends and family members. If you had invested that first $150,000, as opposed to parting ways with it, that amount could have grown to over $4.4 million by the time you turned 65 years old—setting yourself up for the rest of your life. It is ok to share your wealth. In fact, most people have that desire. But remember that money was left to you for a reason, and it is your responsibility to yourself and those who divested it to you to be accountable with it.

Conversely, I've seen women in their mid-twenties receive large inheritances who are too scared to touch it. Sometimes these women listen to professional advice and invest in a way that isn't overly aggressive, and the outcomes set them up for the rest of their lives. Remember that inflation can diminish any money that is not wisely invested. It is ok to take a conservative approach to investing, but make sure that decision is driven by something other than fear.

So what's a girl to do when she is young and comes into a lot of money? Here are some rules I tell my clients:

- Don't go on a spending spree. Resist the urge to spend it unnecessarily.

- Don't give it away, no matter who is asking.
- Talk to a grief counselor, if needed. It's important to separate emotions from finances.
- Work with a financial planner to help manage the money and strategically invest it.

Inheriting money in your twenties has its emotional strains, but it also propels you into a great spot to begin planning for your future. You are literally outpacing your colleagues and will start playing the game with a big lead. By saving and investing wisely, you have a head start on saving for retirement and financial freedom, as you have more time to save and more time to become comfortable with managing your financial assets. The nerves many women feel when receiving an inheritance can be overwhelming, but it is important to remember that you received the money for a reason—honor your loved one by making it work for you and your future.

Chapter 6

YOUR THRIFTY 30'S:
BECOMING ESTABLISHED

❧❦❧

Before Walking Down the Aisle, Forge a Path for the Future

For many people, your roaring twenties are your time to grow into an adult. And if you are lucky, it may also be a chance to meet the individual with which to share the rest of your life. Marriage can change everything, and although you may not consider it when you say your "I do's" or even walk down the aisle, the financial situation you are marrying into and bringing to the table will almost certainly become a monumental part of the equation.

In the midst of discussing cake flavors, choosing dress colors, and considering honeymoon destinations, there's one more important conversation that couples need to have before their wedding day: The Money Talk.

Couples should be talking about money before getting married for a variety of reasons. Not only because it can help them avoid future stress and arguments over finances, but also because it's simply one of the most important, and most overlooked, parts of the wedding planning process. Part of merging your life with that of another person means merging your finances as well. The sooner a couple starts aligning their goals, the better.

Start by having a frank discussion with your partner before combining your finances. This is a big conversation and it will be one of the largest indications of how you interact as a couple. The key is to make sure all major life issues have been addressed through asking plenty of questions: some broad and others more specific. These questions will differ from couple to couple based on several factors, including age at the time of marriage and whether this is a first or successive marriage for either side. The goal is to identify what's important to each partner, both short-term and long-term, be it money for travel, early retirement, or leaving an inheritance to children. Have the conversations now so you can reduce potential stress and the risk of conflict later.

Moreover, ask yourselves what goals the two of you share. For example, a couple hoping to start a family should address not just when they hope to conceive, but where they hope to live, and whether or not one parent will stay at home. If so, which parent? When will this transition take place? No matter what the decision, there will ultimately be an impact on the financial stability of the marriage.

Another aspect of shared finances that's often overlooked is the role of each person's money personality. For instance, if one person is a saver and the other partner a spender, there are bound to be issues down the road; we don't automatically change our habits post-marriage. The same is true if both parties are spenders.

That leads me to a final point that may seem more specific than the others, but in my years of experience, I've come to believe there is no benefit to a couple opening a joint line of credit.

Every individual has their own credit profile, and when entering into a joint credit agreement, there is a primary and a secondary credit holder. Only the primary signer will build credit, or conversely, lose ground if the account falls behind. Instead, each partner should build their own credit in their own name and keep the lines separate, thus strengthening the couple's overall financial picture. In the spirit of a newly married couple, you simply want to celebrate and share everything. But because you have no clue what life has in store, always remember that building and maintaining good credit is extremely important to your individual and collective financial security.

When completed in earnest, pre-wedding financial planning can help couples steer clear of some of the most common financial, and emotional, issues faced in relationships today. Plus, the process is easily replicated from one life goal to the next, creating a road map that two people can continue to navigate together.

Got a Prenup?

Getting married will surely be one of the happiest times of your life. And navigating your marriage will not only be exciting and covered in celebratory moments, but will also require endless communication between you and your loved one. And many of these conversations should be had before you actually tie the knot. Remember to plan now to prevent future problems or miscommunication later. One of the conversations that should be had before you actually tie the knot is directed at a financial split, in the off chance things don't work out.

Money Queen Fact: Only 18% of families headed by single mothers have financial security.[18]

No one wants to talk about a prenup. Certainly, you don't want to be the one to bring it up. But it is a necessary conversation to have. It is not forecasting that a marriage will end, and should not even be viewed as a negative discussion. The reality is that there is no predicting tomorrow and it is an important conversation to have today. So take the time to protect your assets and peace of mind with a prenuptial agreement (prenup).

The idea of a prenup may conjure all sorts of negative images in people's minds. For some, it seems like the hallmark of an unstable union, a couple with a lack of trust or longevity, keeping their assets separate in the midst of a "quickie" marriage. Others think first of greed, while others, still, might just see prenuptial agreements as another "P" word associated with celebrities, like Paparazzi or Paleo Diets.

We talk quite a bit about the emotions of financial planning. A financial contract entered into before marriage is a perfect example of how the two intersect in a very abrupt and sudden manner. The very mention of a prenup can cause feelings of anger and distrust…it's a loaded term with a bad rap. However, the truth is that while a prenuptial agreement can be a sign of trouble ahead, it doesn't have to be.

Taken at face value, a prenuptial agreement commonly refers to provisions for division of property and spousal support in the event of a divorce or breakup of the marriage. Sometimes, a prenup includes provisions for forfeiture of assets on certain conditions as well. From a practical standpoint, a prenuptial agreement is similar to any other financial planning document, in that it prepares for the future and creates a "plan B" in the event it's ever needed. In short, a prenup is all about protection. Divorces, even if uncontested, can cost thousands of dollars. If contested and fueled by emotions, they can cost hundreds of thousands of dollars, and even more in hurt feelings. A messy divorce can take its toll on the entire family. It can span weeks, months, and even years. And cooler minds rarely prevail. But if you give the time, effort, and thought to the situation when things are calm and unemotional, you may save yourself an enormous amount of heartache and headache.

Because of this focus on protecting assets, couples with equal earning potential and equal assets don't necessarily need a prenuptial agreement in place. It's a construct most frequently used by people of high-net worth, or when there's a notable disparity between one spouse's income and the other's. Assets one partner might inherit later in life, family wealth, and children from a previous union can also come into play.

If this sounds like you, there are some key steps to take when contemplating a prenuptial agreement. The first is to retain an attorney— your own attorney.

Many couples share attorneys, just as they do financial planners, and choose to work through one spouse's lawyer when creating a prenuptial agreement; however, because the whole point of a prenup is to protect individual assets, it only makes sense that their own counsel—one who is well-versed in family law and has only your best interest at the forefront of his mind—represent each party. This will help to ensure the creation of an unbiased and fair split of assets if the two of you decided to part ways.

The same goes for a financial planner, whose primary job will be to help you identify what you ultimately want out of the agreement. Are you looking to preserve a family home in your name? Do you want to avoid taking on your partner's debt? Do you want to protect a burgeoning business? All of these questions will come into play, and the higher the net-worth of the individual, the more important it is to ensure the language of your prenuptial agreement addresses any and all scenarios. So remember that before you sign on the dotted line, spend time with a financial planner and attorney who each have nothing but your best interests in mind.

It's also important to remember that your pre-marital assets prior to marriage aren't subject to division after marriage. If you're worth $1 million before walking down the aisle, you're still worth that million after the fact. But even this rule has its exceptions. For instance, in the case of separate funds used to purchase a residence that later becomes the martial home, or a retirement account that grows during the marriage, most states will view these as marital property, even if purchased with the funds from just one side. Both an attorney and a financial planner will help navigate your financial picture and put an agreement together that's fair to everyone, while ensuring that the resulting contract is mindful of existing assets as well as potential future growth thereof.

Another reason to have good counsel on your side is the number of prenuptial agreements that go on to be contested at the time of a divorce. Any undisclosed or undervalued assets, evidence of coercion of one spouse to sign the agreement, improperly filed paperwork, or signature without legal representation can lead to a prenuptial agreement being voided. Lopsided or unrealistic provisions can negate the agreement as well. Did your spouse gain weight? Change their hair color? Get a new tattoo? Chances are, these kinds of demands won't hold water in court. That being said, taking the time to work with professionals on the frontend can save you enormous stress, both legal and otherwise, on the backend.

If the stigma of instability or greed persists, or if a prenup is still something you equate with celebrity, consider this: prenuptial agreements are increasingly common among high net-worth couples. A recent survey of the *American Academy of Matrimonial Lawyers* found that 73% of its members reported an increase in prenups since 2006. 52% reported more women requesting a prenup, and 36% said pensions and retirement benefits are more commonly cited than ever before. While the emotions involved with making the decision to create a prenuptial agreement are very real, so is another truth: No one wants to be married for their money or divorced only to watch half of it walk out the door.

Money Queen Fact: 77% of women in their 20s expect to self-fund their retirement.[19]

After the Wedding: Marrying your Money

As the excitement of the wedding day, the honeymoon, and the first days of wedded bliss begin to settle into the day-to-day routine of marriage, it's time to revisit the financial planning you started as a couple before walking down the aisle.

Grab your files and folders, pen and paper, and your spouse. Have a seat and—in short—offer each another full financial disclosure.

It sounds daunting, but it doesn't need to be. Take baby steps, drafting net worth statements showing each partner's assets—cash, homes, and retirement accounts—along with budgets, to discern what's coming in, what's going out, and how much money is left in surplus. Finally, list each spouse's liabilities, such as student loans, credit card debt, and any outstanding mortgage or car payments.

Dealing with debt is one of the first tasks you have to tackle as a married couple, and you're not alone. According to the Federal Reserve of Economic Data (FRED), U.S. household debt amounted to $12.9 trillion by the second quarter of 2012.

This is when couples need to check in with their Money Mind™. It's important for couples to understand why they make the money decisions they make, and to talk about those decisions at length. For example, does one partner make money decisions out of fear, striving to avoid further debt or overspending at all times? Is one driven by happiness— using money to live for the moment? Or is a sense of commitment at hand; a desire to take care of family, friends, and responsibilities? You can imagine the conflicts that may arise if one spouse has a fear mindset and the other has a happiness mindset. The same caution stands for couples with similar money minds. Two fear minds may be paralyzed by money, while two happiness minds might drive each other further into debt.

Once debt has been addressed, it's time to move on to discussing savings. There must be a purpose for a couple's savings, and it will feel more concrete for both if savings goals are tied to things they both want. Decide as a couple what your goals will be. Do you hope to buy a home? Purchase a new car? Have children? Go back to school?

Whatever your specific goals are, identify them and begin planning budgets for each goal, in addition to saving for retirement and building an emergency fund. This last step is something I've advised my clients to do, consistently, since the financial crisis of 2008. Our economy is still one that requires we each have a personal safety net.

In the past, you may have been told to save the equivalent of at least three to six months' salary. I recommend a full year. I like to have an extra emergency fund—maybe because I am the original "Designer Bag Lady." I would rather be over cautious than underfunded. A full year of savings is what I needed when I went through my prolonged divorce. If you don't have this fear, then six months should be fine.

With these tasks completed, a roadmap has been created for the coming months and years. Remember to take a moment from time to time to revisit the conversation, assure you're still on track, and that you're always aiming toward shared goals.

Money Queen Fact: Only 11% of women in their 20s are 'very confident' they will be able to fully retire with a comfortable lifestyle.[20]

Non-Traditional Relationships

Up to this point we have mostly considered traditional marriage between a man and a woman. But in recent years, the conversation around unmarried couples, for instance, has also taken an interesting turn as more and more states and countries legalize same-sex marriage. When the Defense of Marriage Act (DOMA) was ruled unconstitutional in 2013, conversations surrounding same-sex marriage were instantly peppered with anecdotes about the 1,138 different rights afforded to married couples by the U.S. Federal government that were not otherwise available to non-married couples. It was a catch twenty-two. You had to get married to obtain these protections, but you were not allowed to get married based on your sexual preference. Once denied these rights, gay couples can now share them with their opposite-sex counterparts if they choose to marry. This has been celebrated as a great step toward equality and progress, but it has also led to a slew of new questions among all unmarried couples: what if we choose *not* to marry?

Indeed, domestic partnerships are a living situation that many couples, both same-sex and opposite-sex, choose over marriage for a variety of reasons, ranging from finances to religion to lifestyle. Since not all states have yet to offer full common-law marriage benefits, this leaves a significant percentage of the population to their own devices to plan for the future as a duo.

The good news is that financial planning resources for domestic partnerships do exist, though not in one tidy bundle. A financial planner should help you and your partner find and organize these benefits by asking a series of questions about your collective life and future together.

Sometimes, these questions are difficult, but they can help guard against potentially disastrous outcomes. For instance, if one partner dies, will the other be able to remain in the same house? What will they receive? Do they have power of attorney? What other issues may arise?

Unmarried couples should also designate their partner as a *health care surrogate,* maintain a joint bank account for shared expenses, and also ensure they are one another's respective emergency contacts on all legal documents. These are just some of the concerns a financial planner can help you address, when you find yourself in need of guidance.

From this point, several creative steps can be taken to safeguard a couple's standard of living and well-being. For example, houses in one person's name can be made the subject of a '*life estate,*' allowing the surviving partner to remain in the home. Another option is to open a life insurance policy in your partner's name. An inexpensive policy— say, the approximate amount it might cost to go out for dinner one night a week—can be enough to provide mortgage or rent and living expenses for a surviving partner in the years following a death. These are just a few examples of the many opportunities available. Speak with a well-informed financial advisor to discuss the entire bundle of options available to you and your partner.

When it comes to love, we all make our own personal choices. But whatever those choices are, it's always important to protect our relationships and ourselves, no matter what form they take.

Most of us are still opting to walk down the aisle and join in marriage with our partner. According to a 2013 Gallup Poll, 65% of U.S. residents aged 35-54 report being currently married. Furthermore, 20% of that group indicates they were previously married.

No matter what the marital statute, all couples should be sure to have that first "Money Talk" about combining finances, and then they should continue to discuss their goals and financial plans well after they've settled into their relationship.

The DOMA Ruling Changes Everything—
Even for Financial Advisors

In a 2013 ruling by The United States Supreme Court, the judges made a decision that will change the lives of many same-sex couples, as well as bring change to the financial rights that were at the heart of the original case. The Court declared the 1996 Defense of Marriage Act (DOMA) unconstitutional in a 5-4 ruling, as it denied married same-sex couples the same benefits that heterosexual couples received. Not only did this decision place same-sex couples on equal footing with their heterosexual counterparts, it is a financial win for those who have been denied benefits in the past.

Since same-sex couples were not considered married, they were not able to receive any financial benefits of marriage. This even applied to singles living together. They were viewed as both straight and married, or not.

Under this monumental ruling, married same-sex couples will now be able to collect over 1,000 spousal benefits they previously were not entitled to under DOMA. These range from income and gift taxes to insurance and death benefits.

However, couples must be married at the State level to qualify for all of the Federal benefits, which means that domestic partnerships and civil unions still may not qualify. And with every passing month, more and more states are beginning to legalize same-sex marriage. The tides are changing and equality is beginning to ring true. Now we can all face the same complicated financial scenarios that were once reserved for traditionally married couples.

There are definitely many more details that still need to be worked out. But as of now, it is up to the State to determine if these couples are even recognized under the law. This is a huge development for financial advisors who have same-sex couples as clients, like myself. Before, most of the planning that financial advisors learned and practiced was tailored to married heterosexual couples. Now, with evolving legislation, we are progressing towards no longer having to work around this issue as long as same-sex couples are legally married. The options are greater and the conversations more in-depth. But both of these lead to additional opportunities and increased saving prospects.

To this point, we should all be kept informed of the changing laws and how they will affect our clients. Are the benefits retroactive? Can they collect benefits from the past three years? We need this information, and quickly, to ensure we are always ahead of the times and can accurately and precisely advise our ever-changing client base.

When choose your financial planner, take the time to interview a few options and confirm they are properly educated on handling the finances of same-sex partners, whether it is a legally recognized marriage or domestic partnership. Accredited Domestic Partnership Advisor^{SM} programs are available for CERTIFIED FINANCIAL PLANNERS™ through The College of Financial Planning. This covers wealth transfers, taxes, retirement planning, and planning for financial and medical end-of-life needs for domestic partners. Whatever the case may be, inquire as to your prospective planner's background and training to confirm he or she has received this specialized training.

Money Queen Fact: 60% of women are more likely than 52% of men to indicate they have not tried to calculate how much they will need to have saved by the time they retire.

With these tasks completed, an even more detailed roadmap has been forged for the coming months and years. From time to time, and since things are always changing, remember to take a moment to revisit the conversation, assure you're still on track, and that you're always aiming toward shared goals. It's important that this remains an ongoing conversation because saving is a fluid project.

And one of the most important pieces to that project is welcoming in a new addition to your family. Your thirties are often a time when you decide to bring a child into this world. Needless to say, this is one of the biggest changes that can enter a couple's life. You will quickly find significant life changes as you close your twenties and enter into your thirties. Often times, marriage, children, and the beginning of your career are just some of the exciting experiences your thirties will bring. It is a time to cement yourself within the foundation of your life and become established, truly training to become an expert within your chosen profession. But it is also a time to accelerate your savings and work to build financial security. In your thirties, your earning ability may rise, but so will your expenses and responsibilities.

It's no secret that having a child (or two or three) is one of the biggest commitments you will ever make in your lifetime. In fact, most decisions of the heart—marriage, children, caring for aging parents—often seem more difficult than other financial decisions that require careful planning. Oddly, information about preparing for these milestones isn't always easy to find. The good news is that planning to start a family simply begins with asking questions. Remember there isn't a prospective parent in the world that doesn't have plenty to ask. If you're thinking about having children, you've probably already started your planning process without even realizing it.

Money Queen Fact: Just one-third of women have a detailed financial plan in place, and, among the youngest segment (ages 25-34), just one in 10 has a financial plan in place.[21]

One of the first questions many people have is whether or not they'll be able to stay home with their baby after birth, and for how long that will be financially feasible. To do so, there must be enough money coming into the household to cover an absence from work. So the first task at hand is to discern from where these funds will be coming.

Be sure to review employee benefits that relate to pregnancy as soon as possible. The *Family and Medical Leave Act* provides up to twelve weeks leave within one year. However, your employer is not mandated to pay your salary, only to offer the same job or a job with equal pay and benefits when you return.

Some companies and states offer short-term disability benefits, which apply to pregnancy, covering all or some of your salary for a period of time. However, the rules vary from state-to-state and firm-to-firm, so it's key to check what's available to you. Even if these benefits are offered to you, short-term disability benefits related to childbirth can still vary in length of coverage, typically from four to twelve weeks. But other options are available. You may have sick leave or vacation saved and can use it to supplement your time off. Regardless, take the time to understand company policy and communicate with your superiors to see what options are available.

Your child's first few weeks are just one small portion of the planning process. As childcare is a huge cost, planning for daycare or even after-school programs and summer camps should begin as soon as possible. Pre-tax and flexible savings accounts are an excellent way to save for these types of expenses. By deducting regular contributions from your paycheck, you can automatically plan for these large and forthcoming expenses. Pre-tax accounts offer an immediate tax benefit that can be used for dependent care, which allows one or both partners to continue working.

Additionally, college planning can seem downright silly when the future student is still in diapers, but it's never too early to start saving for higher education. In fact, it's now recommended that parents begin saving for their child's college expenses at birth, not just to get ahead of mounting costs, but also to help cement their child's attitudes about his or her relationship with money.

Nearly every state offers *529 College Savings Plans,* operated by the state or educational institutions. These plans are designed to help families set-aside funds for future college related expenses. The money is preserved in a tax-free account for 18 years so long as it's used for college. These plans can be pre-paid or set-up as investment accounts (generally the latter is more common) and can help make saving for college a family affair. In fact, parents, grandparents, or other relatives can contribute to the plan over time. Parents-to-be should be tracking when enrollment is open for 529 plans in their state, and budget for regular contributions. In addition, new parents should consider other budgeting concerns covering the entire household: mortgage, food, utilities, taxes, and the works.

Money Queen Fact: One-quarter of women surveyed
are the primary financial decision-makers in their households.[22]

The questions surrounding child rearing and raising your children will start to come fast and furiously. They may feel overwhelming at first, but proper and organized planning can certainly make the process easier. The answers are out there, and there are plenty of options to consider as you move closer to a due date. With a completed financial checklist in hand, you'll soon find yourself asking one question most often, "Why didn't I start the process sooner?"

Our House

As you continue building your life and growing your family, keeping an eye on your finances and determining what they might look like in the future is doubly important. Any carpenter or contractor will tell you that when building a house, the closer to completion you get, the more tasks there will be to finish the project from the floor to the roof. As we grow, the same rings true for our financial lives: things change, course corrections need to be made, and certainly unexpected surprises occur. This analogy couldn't be more appropriate (both literally and figuratively) than in the case of actually buying a home.

In the 2000's, we witnessed a real-estate bubble that led many people to believe their all-American dream home was right around the corner. They made offers and closed quickly, moved into their new houses, and all was well with the world…but only for a matter of years. Shortly thereafter, the bubble burst, the real estate market went into a deep freeze, and our banking system is still shuddering from the aftershocks.

A key reason the housing market imploded was that buyers, and sellers alike, did not follow the tried and true guidelines of home ownership. Debt ratios were stretched to unmanageable levels, and, in many cases, people found they were saddled with mortgages that soon exceeded the value of their homes and their ability to pay for them.

It's imperative to crunch preliminary numbers and gauge where your finances stand before speaking to a realtor or visiting your bank. In fact, your first visit should be to your financial advisor. Whether married or in a domestic partnership, the formula is the same, and it's fairly simple math.

Money Queen Fact: *Fewer than two in 10 women feel "very prepared" to make wise financial decisions. Half indicate that they "need some help," and one-third feel that they "need a lot of help."*[23]

First, combine your annual income with that of your partner, and divide that number by twelve. Then, multiply by .28 (the debt (mortgage) to income ratio percentage). The result is the allowable amount for which you should be able to qualify for a mortgage, principle, interest, taxes and insurance (PITI). This is what is called your debt to income ratio. An example equation is below. For simplicity's sake, we're assuming each partner makes about $50,000 a year:

Partner A $50,000
Partner B $50,000
$100,000 / 12 = $8,333
$8,333 x .28 = **$2,333**

Following the math, this particular couple would qualify for a $2,333 maximum monthly mortgage payment. Now, let's put another set of numbers to work to better understand the total level of acceptable debt: the couple's total monthly income multiplied by .36—in this case, $3,000—subtracting the maximum monthly mortgage payment to determine the acceptable level of additional debt, like car notes and student loans.

Partner A $50,000
Partner B $50,000
$100,000 / 12 = $8,333
$8,333 x .36 = $3,000
- $2,333
$ 667

Take the time to write down these equations and use them as your financial situation guideline. These calculations arm you with hard numbers that relate to your current financial picture—no estimates, no gray areas. It is cut and dry—crystal clear. From this point, the next step is to assess how interest rates will affect your purchase, and that's determined by factoring in your credit rating.

The better your credit score, the better interest rate you'll receive when applying for a mortgage. With a perfect credit score, the lowest annual rate can be yours. As the credit score number falls, though, interest rates rise, positioning someone with a poor credit-score to absorb a very high interest rate.

Finally, plan to put 20% down on a home, when applying for a 30-year fixed mortgage. This will leave you with only 80% of the sale price left to finance, but also enough room to make corrections in the event of a lost job or other family emergency.

As with all financial decisions, careful planning and savings are the most important guideposts on the road to home ownership. These equations prove that there is safety in numbers, and also that the country's collective dream of home ownership is not out of your grasp.

Money Queen Fact: The majority (59%) of women who estimate their financial needs guess what their retirement savings should be rather than using a calculator or advisor.[24]

Divorce

Your thirties welcome in many first time and monumental financial experiences. Most of these are positive. But some, like divorce, can be earth shaking. Now, that is not to say it will end your life and shatter your financial security. It won't—especially if you have a prenup. But in the off chance that you don't, you will still be able to recover if you make smart decisions as you move forward. That brings us to our next lesson: *Whenever you want to resist, persists.* Plans don't always work out the way we want. Instead of resisting the change, it's important to embrace it and go with the flow. Good things can happen when you stick to your guns and follow your gut.

In matters of the heart, things may not turn out the way we'd planned, and we may end up facing divorce. We've already learned how prevalent divorce is in the U.S., and when a marriage fails, it doesn't matter what age you are—it's a painful process. Divorce is also one of the best examples of how emotions and finances can intersect in a potentially catastrophic manner. When it comes to divorce, there is a vast slate of financial questions and concerns in the midst of what might be one of the most difficult periods we'll face in a lifetime.

Along those lines, there is one particular question I hear consistently from women dealing with divorce: *"Will I run out of money?"* To help evaluate this concern, it's important to understand what you'll be up against as soon as possible, so you can begin to weigh reality against your goals for the future. Indeed, the first reality divorcées face is living on lower income. For example, a woman who has a high-earning spouse might go from living in a large home to a smaller house or apartment and, concurrently, have to regroup with a smaller income. She'll need to reevaluate her spending habits, including what she spends on herself or her children, and look into the future toward tomorrow's expenses: college, emergencies, and retirement to just name a few. In fact, this may be the first time she's planned a budget on her own.

The dirty truth is that a woman's financial picture is going to look different than it did before marriage, no matter what the financial specifics are. It's not just a reduction in income that can cause problems; a divorcée who receives an annual lump sum from her ex-spouse may see that influx of cash as an opportunity to do something special with her children, or to make a large purchase such as a home or a car.

But if "living for now" involves borrowing from your life of tomorrow, retirement goals can be quickly thrown off track. Even in good times, different Money Minds will make decisions about finances based on any number of emotions, including fear or the pursuit of happiness. At this point in life, it is vital to continuously run your numbers, revisit financial plans, evaluate how well your savings are accruing and, ultimately, hold yourself accountable for your actions and decisions.

It's not always fun, but it's necessary and will eventually lead to greater peace of mind. Ironically, taking some of the emotion out the equation helps greatly in creating a new plan and, in turn, watching that plan take hold and begin to grow can lead to new feelings of worth. The process doesn't need to be "one more sacrifice." Instead, think of this as delayed gratification, and the first steps toward your new, best life.

Money Queen Fact: The number of older women living in poverty is 50% higher than older men living in poverty.[25]

Move on with your Divorce, and your Mortgage

Now that you've signed the papers and settled the terms, the next important question to answer is: who gets what? Now that you're divorced, you're ready to live your new life away from your ex, but if you got to keep the house, are you really getting away from him? Even though the divorce settlement says the house is all yours, until you and your ex file the necessary paperwork, the other person still legally owns half of your home. That's good to know ahead of time, right?

Even if the divorce was amicable, it is still not a good situation in which to live. What if your ex was the owner of a business, and the business is sued, could they go after your house? In those states that don't have the Homestead Protection Act (where homeowners are protected from having their homes sold to pay off unsecured debts), the answer is *yes.*

You're probably thinking, "So, what's a girl to do to get out of that mess? Refinance my house?" Stop right there. Refinancing can be an ugly process and should be avoided at all times. In fact, there are two weeks' worth of paperwork to even submit the application. It is a painful process no matter who you are or how much money you have in the bank. It's almost like giving your first born to the bank for something you already own.

Plus, it can be expensive! Currently, closing costs for a $350,000 home are roughly $20,000. That's not chump change. And you have to come up with them on the frontend or finance them into the deal. You'll also have to consider long-term costs. Say that your current interest rate on your mortgage is 4%. If you refinance, you'll have to take today's current interest rate of 5%.

For a $300,000 mortgage at 4% interest, your monthly payment is $1,432 per month. A mortgage for the same home at 5% interest will bring your monthly payments to $1,610 per month, which is $178 more each and every month than you were originally paying. Over the life of your 30-year mortgage, that equates to shelling out an additional $64,000 for a home you already own. Seems silly doesn't it? But there may be a better option. A full refinance should be your last choice.

Consider filing a *Quitclaim* as soon as you finalize the divorce papers. A *Quitclaim Deed* is a legal document that your ex, or the owner/grantor, signs to quit or terminate any right they have to the home, which transfers the claim solely to you as the recipient/grantee.

That being said, there are three scenarios in which Quitclaims can be used:

1. **You have no mortgage.** The only thing you need to do is file a Quitclaim Deed to remove your ex from the title.
2. **Both of your names are on the title, while only one (the one keeping the house) is on the mortgage.** Like the first scenario, all you need is a Quitclaim Deed to remove the other from the title and take sole possession.
3. **Both of your names are on the title and mortgage.** In this case, file your Quitclaim Deed to remove the other from the title while keeping their name on the mortgage.

In the third option, it is perfectly common for ex-*spouses* to keep the other's name on the mortgage, even if simply for financial reasons. In some cases, people cannot afford to keep the house on their own, and, depending on the state, can possibly owe additional taxes in order to change the ownership. But, removing your ex from the title or deed is much more important than having him removed from the mortgage. As long as his name is on the title, he still legally owns the property.

But if you do want your ex off the mortgage, you can try to prove to the bank that you've been paying the mortgage single-handedly for at least twelve months. At this point you should be able to ask them for a *Release of Liability*. The lender will run a credit check and ensure that you can afford the mortgage on your own. But keep in mind that you can't use this option if you're underwater. Thankfully, the real-estate market is improving and most people are doing better than a few years ago, so this option may be readily available.

If the *Release of Liability* option doesn't work, another suggestion is to simply play hardball with the bank. If they won't remove your ex from the mortgage, then it's time to leverage refinancing with another lender. The majority of the time, the original bank will do it because they don't want to lose your business.

If all else fails, you can always consider applying for a Loan Modification or Loan Assumption, where you can redo the paperwork in order to completely take the other person off the mortgage. Sometimes people are required to show the divorce settlement to prove intent when using this option. Hopefully, with a little knowledge under your belt and plenty of patience, you can take the proper steps to finally complete the last details of your divorce settlement—and do it all on your terms.

In addition to consulting with a certified financial advisor, consider circling back with your mortgage broker to have a better understanding of what opportunities are financially solvent and available. They can offer the available options and even counsel you on what may be the best financial fit.

Money Queen Fact: Women work an average of 27 years; men work an average of 40.[26]

Job Loss

Your thirties will bring about numerous financial changes. In addition to divorce, there is always the chance you can experience another life-altering experience: job loss. This can be as big a blow as a break-up. Women, in particular, tend to find their passion, their self-worth, and their own strength through their careers. So, losing a position can deal a mighty blow to our self-esteem, as well as to our bottom lines, especially if another source of income is not in the picture.

It's important to note that being laid-off and being fired are, indeed, two different scenarios. For all intents and purposes, a lay-off is when an employee is "let go" for business reasons, such as outsourcing, downsizing, or the closing of the business. A firing is typically termination based on your ability (or inability) to perform your job responsibilities.

Layoffs are all too common these days. Whether it's a few employees losing their jobs due to financial restraints, or the closing of an entire department due to restructuring, economic instability is something that has the ability to trickle down to us when we least expect it. Plus, the worst part about lay-offs is that they aren't your fault. You can work for an employer for over a decade, be a top-performer, and excel at every aspect of your job, but still be at risk for reasons over which you have no control.

One thing lay-offs and firings do have in common is that neither are something you can *exactly* plan for, but you can be prepared if it happens. With that in mind, here are seven steps to regaining your sanity during this tough time:

1. **Relax.** So you just got the news. What do you do now? Breathe, stay calm, and most importantly, *don't flip out.* Don't let your emotions get the best of you, because how you accept the news is very important. As tempting as it may be to get worked up and emotional, it is more important to accept the news graciously and leave on good terms. This reflects well on you and gives you some options in the long run. You never know if you could get hired back or need a reference in the future. Accept it and move on. It is going to happen if you go down graciously, or in a ring of fire.

2. **Check your emergency fund.** I am a firm believer in having for an emergency fund for times like this. As previously discussed, plan to have three-to-six month's worth of income stashed away to buy you some time. Some companies offer severance pay, which can range from two-weeks to two-month's pay (or more) and may or may not include benefits. Severance packages vary by employer, and some don't offer one at all. Take as much as you can get, including any career counseling, resume writing, and/or any re-training offered. And remember that severance pay is negotiable and there is no harm in asking for a little bit more than you are being offered.

3. **File for unemployment.** While this isn't mandatory, it certainly helps. Check with your state unemployment agency for all the necessary information. But keep in mind there are restrictions and rules to follow. The government set this program up for times like this, so take advantage of it while you can. The Department of Labor is a good place to start. If given the

opportunity to resign or be terminated, always resign. That simple act may keep you eligible for unemployment benefits.

4. **Settle your insurance coverage.** COBRA is a government program that extends your insurance coverage for up to 18 months. If you decide to take this route, it is vital that you get a certificate from your (former) employer with a date of separation as soon as possible because there is a 60-day window in which to file. In addition to your health insurance, you will also lose your disability and life insurance if you get them through your employer. Now is the time to decide whether or not you need either type and if you should invest in a private policy.

5. **Rollover your 401(k).** Lay-offs often lead to feelings of bitterness, which is why most people wouldn't want keep their hard-earned money at the place that just let them go. Your 401(k) is something you've worked hard to build, so you should transfer it into a traditional IRA, and then to a new 401(k) plan (if applicable) when you find a new job. Make sure you file the necessary paperwork as you are headed out of the door to ensure all the loose strings are tied up.

6. **Don't waste money.** Avoid spending money if you don't have to. It's vital that you get serious, set a budget, and stick to it. Every penny counts when you're out of work. You never know when your next paycheck will arrive, so do your best to be as conservative as possible.

7. **Sit down with a financial planner.** There is no time like the present to re-evaluate your financial life. Talk with your advisor to see how the job loss will affect your family and future plans, and then work together to set a course of action for the next few months.

Money Queen Fact: *Two-thirds of all working women earn less than $30,000 a year in jobs without pensions.*[27]

At first, it may be difficult to cope with losing your job. But it is important to remember that things will eventually turn around. So, stay positive best you can as you navigate this difficult process. Remember you've been given the gift of time to do what you want to do, and also on your own terms. Don't automatically assume that losing your job is entirely a bad thing. Sometimes it can be a blessing in disguise, and a moment in time to take inventory of your life and do some self-exploration and evaluation.

As always, start by asking yourself some questions:

Are you happy with your career?

Do you need a change?

Do you need to spend more time with your family?

Take the time to answer these questions so you are clear on where to go from here. Your next move should be well considered and well analyzed to ensure it will be a lasting one.

Chapter 7

YOUR FANTASTIC 40'S: WHAT'S NEXT?

S o you made it through your thirties in one piece? You've either dodged or survived divorce, job loss, and maybe even the birth of a couple of children. As they enter their forties, many women will find themselves asking questions about what employment will look like for them moving forward. In other words, *who's the boss*? Is it you, or someone else? There comes a time in many people's careers when they consider self-employment, and the shock of losing a job often acts as a catalyst for those people who've long dreamed of working for themselves. In the same way, it can also signal to someone who's not sure about working for herself that being part of a team at a larger outfit is a better choice.

The thirties are a time to cement your position in your respective industry so you can spend your forties at the pinnacle of your career. Big decisions can be made, like accepting a new position or raise within your company, or accepting a lateral move, or even starting your own business. Since the first opportunities are pretty self-explanatory and overall carry little risk, let's take some time to focus on going out on your own.

Leaving the corporate grind to start a new business or sole proprietorship is a transition that works quite well for some, but it isn't for everyone. I tell my clients who are thinking about becoming self-employed to go ahead and contemplate the future; after all, we're working toward creating their one best financial life together, and that starts with setting goals. After being in corporate America for ten years, I started my own firm in my thirties. It was very difficult. No one told me it would take working seven days a week for over five years to really turn it into something special. I started slow, with just two clients my first year. But my client base and my earnings grew.

Luckily, I planned well and had a large reserve of cash from my previous job to sustain me though this period. There were many times I wanted to quit. But I was determined. I have seen clients of mine try to start their own businesses before they had the necessary cash reserves or experience to really do so. I've seen them work hard only to pay to go to work. Starting your own business and going out on your own is not for everyone. Before you make that exciting but pivotal move, there are a couple of questions to ponder at the start of this conversation:

- **Who will go with me?** This question will help anyone considering self-employment to predict what the early months of her new business will look like. The most important aspect of starting any business is in knowing how to gain and retain clients, and it takes considerable time to build a client base if you're starting from zero. Ask yourself which clients or customers may follow you once you've left your current firm. Is your reputation strong enough to woo them away from a larger outfit? Does the current firm offer incentives to clients that you won't be able to maintain? Are there restrictions on working with current clients once you've left the company? Ensure that there are no non-compete clauses in your contract before even considering a move that will include current clients. And if there are, consult with an attorney to confirm whether or not they are reasonable and enforceable. When starting a new business, the last place you want to be is in lawsuit territory.

- **How will I be paid?** The first hurdle of self-employment is getting people to hire you; the second is getting them to part with their hard earned money. The days of a weekly paycheck will be gone, and there may be unpredictable rises and falls in income, especially at the start. Because of the uncertainty, getting paid is also about retaining the assets you currently have while simultaneously increasing them.

The risks associated with start-up and operating costs need to be weighed, and boy, are there ever costs. Regardless of your profession, self-employment means you've just become a one-woman shop. There are phones, software, and office supplies to purchase. You are the sales, marketing, and IT departments. In the beginning, you may answer the phones, schedule your calendar, and even get the coffee for potential clients. You need to keep the place clean. You *will* be taking out the garbage. But that is just the nature of starting a business.

To get started, create a list of needs that will draw on your resources, talent, and time—everything from a web designer to paper towels and tea bags. Note what can be outsourced and what will stay in-house. For instance, can you manage bookkeeping alone? If billing, collection, and accounting aren't handled correctly, it's likely that you will lose money.

I also recommend six to twelve months (or more) of emergency funds to weather fluctuations in income as you start your business.

While that may be difficult for many people, it's a recommendation that grew from the reality that most new businesses operate at a loss in their first few months. It's not just a cushion to cover expenses, but also an added protection for the business in its early stages.

The process of going it alone is daunting and can be downright scary at times. But if approached carefully, the rewards are what most people seek: flexibility, self-reliance, creative freedom, and the reality of financially benefiting from successes. These are goals worth setting. But remember to start with a well-considered and thought out plan. Only then will you position yourself to navigate the rough terrain in the most efficient manner possible.

Returning to the Workforce

For some women, the forties are a time where they find themselves actually returning to the workforce. Because of a divorce, fully grown children, or even the desire to save just a little bit more for retirement, many women decide to jump back into the workforce as they journey through their fantastic forties. Women often exit the workforce for many different reasons, Military service, childcare, pursuing an advanced degree, illness…these are all valid reasons for leaving the workforce. Financial concerns, a move, or simply the desire to return to work are popular motives behind why some resume a well-heeled career, or even start a brand new one.

Still, re-launching a career after an absence is a big worry, especially for women. We might ask ourselves: "Are my skills too rusty? Am I still relevant? Can I jump into a new job as easily as I did five, 10, or 20 years ago?"

Money Queen Fact: Most (65%) Baby Boomer women do not have a backup plan if forced into retirement sooner than expected.[28]

As with any life planning decisions, asking these questions can be daunting, but they are a great place to start. The next step is using the information we glean through those questions to plot a course for the future. Consider the following five tips for reigniting a career, and making sure the 'launch' goes smoothly:

1. **Prepare for Launch.** Even before you're fully ready to re-enter the workforce, a few proactive steps each year can help to significantly ease the difficulty of re-entry down the road. Keep up with industry trends, attend a networking event or two, and stay in touch with colleagues and mentors. Then, when it's time to consider returning to work, analyze and consider all facets of your decision:

   - What is your appetite for a career?
   - What are your childcare or elder care responsibilities?
   - What sort of support do you have from your spouse, family, and friends?
   - Some people may need to accept a cut in pay and title— are you prepared to move down a few rungs on the career ladder, or to move a step back in order to take two steps forward?

   As the right time approaches, immerse yourself more fully in your field of choice. Subscribe to industry publications, browse professional websites, sign up for a college class or two, attend conferences and lectures in your field and do everything you literally can to amass the knowledge, skills, and professional vocabulary that will mark you as a serious contender for top jobs.

2. **Create a "Re-entry" Resume.** Many people find it challenging to prepare a resume after being home for several years. The key here is to develop a "re-entry" resume that highlights

strengths, downplays chronological breaks in work experience, and addresses unique challenges head-on. In other words, a re-entry resume focuses on skills and experience, rather than using the dates of past employment to organize important information. Include volunteer work, project work, freelance work, or anything that shows you are using skills that are valued in your industry or in the workplace. Include information that communicates you have improved skills and stayed current in your industry. Make sure that you are up-to-date on the technology required for your field, check to see that you are not using outdated terminology, and that you are including updated industry language.

3. **Develop your Flight Plan.** The notion that there's only one-way to enter (or re-enter) the workforce is a thing of the past. For example, even internships have evolved to include "returnships" for those returning to the workforce. Essentially, returnships are offered to experienced workers who have taken time off as a way to reintroduce them to today's workplace and to polish their skills. Like most internships, returnships are usually short stints at a company for little or no pay, with the goal of building important resume skills. If such a position isn't available, volunteering for a cause that you're interested in or are passionate about is another way to put your existing skills to work and learn new things. Finally, if you're not already using social media to fuel your job or volunteerism search, start now. Sites such as LinkedIn, Facebook, and Twitter are vital to making connections and learning about new opportunities in today's workforce. Your know-how in this area is one more important bullet point to mention on resumes and in interviews, as well.

4. **Maintain Communication.** Experts estimate that as many as 80% of all job offers are the result of networking activity

rather than the traditional job application process. Some people who've been absent from the workforce for some time may think their network has disappeared, but we all still have one in place. Remember to reach out to friends and contacts from many different sectors of your life, including former colleagues, and also school contacts, college or graduate school alumni groups, places of worship, extracurricular activities (for yourself or children), sports teams, neighbors, and even the local coffee shop. You truly never know from where that next great connection will originate. Learn from those who have made a transition and talk with others who are in the same stage. Have business cards printed up. Contact cards with a little flair are fine if you're not comfortable claiming a specific title for yourself. Develop a brief elevator pitch and begin to look for industry events in your area to test it out. Essentially, you're making it your job to find a job.

5. **Make Contact.** It is a great idea to practice interviewing if you have been out of the loop for a while. Remember to be positive about your experiences and your excitement about returning to work. Do not apologize for being away, instead be confident about the timing of your decisions to focus on family and return to outside work. Assure potential employers you are returning to work not because you have to, but because you want to. Make sure that your interview attire and attitudes are both current. An applicant should be able to not only explain a break in their job experience, but also explain how that break might actually enhance their resume. A candidate with military experience, for example, may have gained management, procurement, logistics, and technology skills. Someone returning to work after rearing a family can bring communication, organization, and marketing experience. Charitable work can encompass financial

management, budgeting, public relations, and fundraising. All of these skills are transferable, and all of them can benefit any organization.

More Re-launch Resources

Consider some additional re-launch resources that can be helpful as you begin the exciting road to reentry:

- **www.irelaunch.com.** This site supports mid-career professionals, as well as the companies and organizations that want to hire them. They offer programs, events, and content for individuals and employers. It also includes a list of companies and colleges/universities that offer specific programs for women returning to the workforce.
- **www.encore.com.** A website devoted to supporting baby boomers who wish to combine personal fulfillment, social impact, and continued income, so they can put their passion to work for the greater good. Includes job listings and links to other job listing sites.
- **www.retirementjobs.com.** Free to jobseekers, this site seeks to identify and qualify companies most suited to older workers. Includes job listings and articles of interest.
- **www.aarp.org.** Contains "work and retirement" section with helpful articles on finding a job, life at work, and re-careering.

The Second Time Around

By this point, the idea of planning until you can't plan anymore should be embedded deep into your brain. And with that notion, you should also be simultaneously aware of the value in consistently analyzing and evaluating along the way. Remember, it is a fluid journey for us all. What works today may not work tomorrow. And what worked yesterday may not be the best decision for today. For better or worse, change is the only constant in life, and it's just going to keep popping up its head to say hello like a pesky relative. While some change like divorce is no fun for anyone, let me assure you that finding new love is one of the best things you can experience in your life.

Money Queen Facts: Nearly 1/3 of women between the ages of 40 and 69 "can't estimate" how much money they can withdraw annually from their retirement accounts.[29]

As we move forward, our own ideas about love and relationships evolve along with the circumstances surrounding them. Such is the case when you're about to blend your family with your new partner's family after remarrying. This is one of the most interesting and unique experiences you may ever find during your forties. In fact, creating the *Brady Brunch* is probably a topic not nearly discussed enough. Honestly, when you think about blending families, doesn't your mind go straight to *The Brady Bunch* and the three girls and three boys who immediately got along and started calling one another 'brother' and 'sister'? That perfect TV family was, well, made for TV. In real life, it is rarely that effortless and ideal. Now that doesn't mean that blending families is a recipe for disaster. It is not. In fact, it can be a very exciting change in your life. But it will call for thought and planning, not just dropping everyone in a room and pushing the "easy" button.

In real life, blending families can be a stressful time. Not only are you and your significant other about to begin your new life together, but you also have to worry about children, finances to combine, and estates to plan. Juggling everything is no simple task, but with a little planning and forethought, it can be close to harmonious, although perhaps not to the point at which your new brood starts a successful family band.

Like I tell all of my clients, it is vital that you and your partner discuss your finances before walking down the aisle or even before getting engaged, and a later-in-life marriage or domestic partnership is no exception. In fact, based on the accumulation of wealth and sheer property over the years, it can be twice as important and twice as involved. Every couple's situation is different, but here are some of the major topics that most people need to know about ahead of time:

- **Do either of you have any debt?** Full disclosure here is key. Be honest with one another, as the truth will eventually prevail and create problems later if you did not divulge all of your personal information.

- **What are your views on savings?** Some people like to save everything, while others are spenders. You both need to be on the same page in order to build your future together. A quick discussion to pinpoint your tendencies can often do the trick.

- **Do you need a prenup?** This can be a touchy subject for some couples, but can be important to help spell out specific plans. I've laid out some more information on prenuptial agreements above. Remember, prenups are simply planning mechanisms without emotions in case the two of you decide to go in a different direction.

- **Do you have mutual financial goals?** There is no time like the present to align your goals. It wouldn't hurt to talk to a financial planner to begin preparations for your financial future and start the planning process.

- **What is the moving situation?** Merging two families requires merging households, both in location and in structural makeup. Decide ahead of time if you will move into the other's home, or get a new one altogether. Aim to be fair, as the buying and selling of homes could have big financial outcomes.

After you've laid the groundwork for your financial future together, it's time to think about the other large and very important aspect of your lives: your families. Blending families is challenging, but it is important to remember that there are other people, kids, in-laws, etc., for whom you may be responsible. Here are a few guidelines that I always recommend to my clients as they begin to fold two different dynamics together:

1. **Establish the ground rules early.** Be upfront with your children and stepchildren about what will change, both in small ways like who will be living in the home, and in big ways, such as what will happen to their inheritance. After all, not everyone likes surprises. Keeping your children informed now will save everyone the stress and hurt feelings in the long run.

2. **Keep everything equal.** You can't play favorites with your children and stepchildren. Biological or not, everything must be equal and fair. From allowances to special rules, all of the children need to receive the same treatment, regardless of what they received before the two families became one.

3. **Consider your parents.** Do you and your spouse have aging parents? Besides taking care of the kids, it's also important to decide who is responsible for taking care of them—sooner rather than later. There can be substantial financial impact on caring for an elderly or sick relative, so ensure you are square on who will be paying the bills and how the care will be provided.

4. **Agree upon household roles and responsibilities.** Who is responsible for the bills and the housework? Set up the ground rules as soon as you merge the families together. Are you both responsible for the bills? Then set up a joint checking account. Do you want everyone, even the kids, to pitch in with the housework? Then set up a cleaning schedule, or whatever works for your new family.

5. **Protect your future.** What will happen when a spouse dies? If not planned right, stepchildren could be disinherited, so plan ahead of time to protect your children. Update your estate plan and will as soon as you are married to establish what will happen in case of future tragedy. This is also a good time to reevaluate your life insurance coverage and make sure you are properly protected and funded.

Having come from a blended family myself, I can say from experience that blending families aren't easy, but approaching it the right way can mean the world of difference for both the parents and the children. Make sure you are upfront about your current financial and family makeup; be honest, and most importantly, be fair and consistent.

Chapter 8

YOUR FABULOUS 50'S: AVOIDING THE LANDMINES

The Empty Nest

At this point in your life, you've probably spent the better part of the past two decades raising and caring for your kids—you were their chauffeur, personal chef, maid, nurse, and tutor—and now they've moved on to college or are starting lives of their own. It can feel as if a big piece of your life, and the reasons for many of your daily responsibilities, are gone.

Welcome to the club, empty nester. You are certainly not alone. At some point in their lives, all parents reach this stage and everyone handles it differently. Some are devastated, while others count down the days until the kids move out. It's important to remember that you control how the situation is handled, so why not make it a positive one?

First things first: What are you going to do with your newfound freedom? This is a great time to recreate yourself. After all, you are a different person from who you were before you had children. Sit down, look in the mirror, and ask yourself this question, *"What do I want my future to look like?"* For some women, the answer is they want to go back to work. Whether full or part time, rejoining the work force is a great way to get used to your new life without the kids, while also earning extra income to live on or save for retirement.

Money Queen Fact: 45% of women work part-time, and are less likely to have workplace retirement benefits.[30]

Others choose this time in life to start their own business. Often, this decision grows from a hobby that can be turned into a successful business now that you may have more time to devote to it. If you're not keen on returning to your career, or if you're not sure what you want to do, volunteerism is a great way to stay engaged with the community as well as identify your strongest skills and passions. There are plenty of organizations that need manpower, plus you'll earn karma-points in the game of life.

Finally, if none of these options appeal to you, or if you still find yourself with time on your hands, find a hobby. Whether it's taking up tennis or yoga, it's never too late to learn a new skill or trait. Filling your free time with activities that make you feel fulfilled and productive is a key aspect in evaluating what your purpose is and where your life is headed. Although it's important to remind yourself that this is an exciting time, it can also be stressful. Thus, it certainly doesn't hurt to talk to someone and ensure you are clear and organized regarding your overall goals and newfound time.

On the road to your new life, friends and family are a great resource with which to start. They offer great advice and generally look out for your best interests. The other important people in your life can also offer a shoulder to lean on. But for whatever reason, if you feel like you need some more objective guidance, visiting a counselor can do a world of good and can help you cope with your feelings about your new life situation.

Life Coaches are another option. They are specially trained to help you get on track to meet your goals. They can be fantastic sounding boards, offer valuable feedback, and even push you in a direction you never before considered.

Finally, if I've said it once, I've said it a thousand times: visiting a Financial Planner can help you plot out a course for the future. One of the first questions a financial planner will ask at this stage in your life is: *Are you paying for your children's education, or have they cut all the financial strings?* The answer will point both your advisor and yourself in the direction toward feasible, achievable goal setting. They may help you structure your current and realistic financial environment so you can make a job or volunteer decision based not only on what you want to do, but also on what you need to do.

You may or may not know the answer right away, and that is completely natural. But having frank discussions will help you decide where you want to go. Starting the process will also give you a new sense of purpose and the knowledge that your time is worthwhile.

Just because your children have moved out doesn't mean your life stops. Just remember that this is a new chapter in your life, so make the most of it!

Imagine this. You've saved for years to create a nest egg to carry you through retirement. You're no Rockefeller, but you've done well and feel as if financial security is within reach. *If only it was just a bit more,* you think, you could be set for everything you need and want in your Golden Years. You can sail away into the sunset and not think twice about financial stability for the rest of your life.

And then your prayers are answered. A friend gets in touch with a great idea that's already made her money—just about the same sum you were looking to add to your hard-earned retirement fund. It's working for her, so you decide to make an investment. I always say, "If it sounds too good to be true, it probably is." Even though your gut tells you otherwise, you still decide to move forward with what can only be viewed as a "get rich quick" scheme. Returns are great for a few months, but cracks start to show in the agreement. Payments are smaller, statements are less detailed, and phones are being answered less frequently at the parent office: Something's up, and it's not good. You can feel that something is gravely wrong.

And then your greatest fears become a reality. It's not long before you realize you've been pulled into the dark side of money management: the dreaded Ponzi scheme. In a matter of months, decades of savings have dwindled to almost nothing.

Ponzi schemes have been around for centuries, even before the man they're named for was ever born. The name 'Ponzi Scheme' was first coined in the early 1900s after Charles Ponzi, an Italian émigré living in Massachusetts, who devised a plan to make money from the sale of International Reply Coupons, a sort of 'Postage Paid' option of the day that allowed recipients of mail to reply to the sender at no cost to themselves. Varying rates of postage around the world meant these coupons could often be sold for profit in the U.S., and after discovering weaknesses in the system, Ponzi soon began pitching the idea to friends and colleagues.

It worked, for a while. His investors made money as promised, and Ponzi was swimming in it. But it wasn't long before he was "borrowing from Peter to pay Paul," using later investors' buy-ins to pay returns to existing investors, and operating in the red. Eventually the funding would disappear and so would the initial investment.

Sadly, Ponzi's story has been echoed in nearly every other such scheme that followed: promises of great returns followed, eventually, by insolvency that leaves investors completely wiped out. The only real difference is that the sums lost have become more and more dire. For example, in 2008 when Bernie Madoff's Ponzi scheme collapsed, it robbed investors of nearly 18 billion dollars—more than 53 times the losses caused by Ponzi (who also brought down six banks in his wake).

So with all the information and disclosures available to investors, how can Ponzi schemes still persist? The answer is that unfortunately, not all Ponzi Schemes are easy to spot. Often, countless hours of work and diligence are put into making these shoddy dealings look legitimate—as much as would go into building a reputable business. Many times, the average investor just won't see any red flags because they've been deftly hidden by flashy websites, promising presentations, and professional looking documents. And even more so, people want to believe these schemes are the real thing.

Once victimized, it leaves investors with a terrible feeling of loss, helplessness, and of deceit. But if you have ever been a victim of a Ponzi scheme, rest assured you are not alone. In 2010, the U.S. government established an interagency Financial Fraud Enforcement Task to investigate and prosecute financial crimes under the code "Operation Broken Trust." By December 2010, "Operation Broken Trust" had identified more than 120,000 people who were defrauded collectively of close to $8 billion through their unwitting involvement in 231 separate cases.

It's a nasty business, but there are several things investors can do to protect themselves. Your first level of protection comes with expert advice, from Certified Financial Planners®, attorneys, and CPAs. If you don't have at least one of those three, you probably shouldn't be investing at this level yet. Reputable investments require a certain level of sophistication, and Ponzi's prey on a lack thereof.

Money Queen Fact: The key to preparing effectively for your "golden years" is knowledge.

On the other hand, financial professionals have not only the expertise, but also an obligation to research any and all investment opportunities their clients bring to them, and to report anything they deem suspicious as part of their corporate duty. They are regulated and carry a fiduciary duty to their clients that leads to accountability. Start by checking the status of any investment firm on the Financial Industry Regulatory Agency's (FINRA) website and ask for referrals and reviews. The Financial Planning Association also offers an exhaustive checklist of questions to review with the help of a financial planner, who will help you sniff out anything rotten.

Another hallmark of Ponzi Schemes is the use of current investors to recruit new ones; that means it could very well be a trusted friend, co-worker, or even an organization such as your church that first brings the opportunity to your attention. That smokescreen of trust is a part of the fraud. Remember, even if an investment does work out for a friend, it still might not work for you.

Beware of big, sweeping statements in both conversations and literature about an investment: phrases like "you can't lose," or "you'll double your money in six months" can be signs of trouble ahead. Look at the company's website, too. Is it lacking contact information or asking you for a large amount of personal detail? The same goes for actual investment documents from the outfit. They will probably look very professional, but the warning signs include a lack of details, inflated numbers, or few references to reputable third-party custodians or government bodies. You should always be able to see what's going on with your money: the investments should be easily tracked on your statements and there should always be an independent way to verify the statement through sites like *Yahoo! Finance* or *Big Charts*.

Sooner or later, all Ponzi Schemes fail. But unfortunately, new ones are always popping up. Use your professional network to vet every investment opportunity that comes your way, and your due diligence will protect your hard-earned money from greedy hands. More than anything, remember that there are no "get rich quick" schemes out there that work. Building financial security is an organic process that takes time and effort. It calls for education, information, and understanding; it is truly a game of inches and not a game of yards.

The Good Advice You Just Didn't Take

For each of us, we are hopeful that we surround ourselves with confidants and experts that offer sound, quality advice. We've all been there—that time when you get a sage piece of wisdom and take it for granted. We didn't realize it at the time, but in hindsight, the writing was clearly on the wall. Naturally, we all regret ignoring great advice, especially when the outcome isn't what we expected.

Alanis Morissette summed up this situation perfectly in her song "Ironic" when she said, *"It's the good advice that you just didn't take."* In my line of work, I see this situation all too often. I try to give my clients the best advice I can, but it's their choice whether or not to actually take it. Unfortunately they often don't. Now, that doesn't mean I am always right. But I have worked hard to become an expert in my field and to ensure I can offer insightful and valuable advice that I am hopeful my clients will at least consider as they make their financial decisions.

As a financial planner, I have to stay within certain legal boundaries. I can't cross certain lines in hopes that my clients will chose the option that is truly best for them. Sure, I can recommend counseling or contact family members to help influence them, but legally I'm stuck. This is when it gets frustrating, as I sometimes have to watch my clients—some of whom I've known for years—ruin their financial futures against my best advice.

Money Queen Fact: Over 40% of women believe that being financially independent would make them intimidating and unattractive to men, and a third believe it can alienate other women.[31]

Take for instance, a widow, whose husband had a six-figure job and who had $2 million set-aside for retirement. They had a lovely, multimillion-dollar home that cost thousands of dollars each month to maintain. But now that the husband had passed, she could no longer afford to maintain the home and, against my advice, refused to sell it. Slowly but surely, keeping this house was eating through her retirement fund and there was nothing else I can do. My hands were tied and while she did not see it at the time, she was quickly headed in the wrong direction.

Greed also plays a major role in why some people make poor choices. I've seen many people being taken advantage of by others; but they cannot see the forest for the trees because they were so enamored in their relationship. Grieving widows always seem to be targets for greedy men.

One such widow recently received $1million after her husband passed away. No sooner did she receive the money, than a new man coincidentally came into the picture. Then the erratic spending commenced. Naturally she disregarded my advice to dump the boyfriend and see a counselor, and has since lost everything because of legal trouble that the new boyfriend dragged her into.

Although it seems like something out of daytime drama, I've seen my clients be taken in all sorts of ways. Consider the example of one of my clients who literally joined a cult. In this instance, a $700,000 portfolio turned into $300,000 after taxes and fees, and the cult leader stole the remaining $300,000 for personal use. After not hearing from my client for well over a year, she finally came back—of sound mind—and apologized for not taking my advice. Thankfully, we were able to recover her stolen money and she is now slowly rebuilding her portfolio and financial security.

Fortunately, not all cases are so drastic and dramatic. On a daily basis, we are not dealing with cults or complicated Ponzi schemes. The reality is that the most common cases involve those who don't do anything with their money at all. As much as I try to explain that putting their money in a portfolio will actually *make* them money, they are just too scared to do anything with it. So they just enter a stage of paralysis by analysis. Their inability to make any decision results in making the worst decision of all—doing nothing.

It is frustrating to know that my clients, all of whom I care about, are making uninformed and emotional decisions, and I can't move them to positive action. I don't want my clients to make the same mistakes I see all the time, but there's only so much a Certified Financial Planner™ can do.

But it is not all bad news. Part of the joy of my job is watching my clients grow fortunes and build financial security from the ground up. It is truly something special when my clients see the light and we are perfectly positioned to work together and build a great future for each and every one of them.

Caring for Elderly Parents

As you enter your fifties, most of your parents will be past the age of retirement, and entering the last decade of their lives. Medical concerns and living scenarios should be considered and planned. Luckily, more Americans are living well into their 70's and even into their 80's. But that presents an entirely new set of concerns and conversations their children should have. What happens when an aging parent can no longer care for herself?

Money Queen Fact: 60% of women in their 60's expect to rely on Social Security.

Oftentimes, her children step in and take responsibility for her care. Of the children who do step up, more often it is women who take over caring for their elderly family members. Here are a few more facts:

- This is the first time in history that American couples have had more parents to care for than children.
- Today, the average American woman can expect to spend 18 years caring for an older family member, compared to 17 for her children.
- Almost 40% of all U.S. workers are more involved with caring for a parent than a child.

As you can see, the odds are high that you may be required to care for an aging parent at some point in your life. It may happen in your fifties, it could happen sooner. But planning early on can certainly make a big difference when it is time to act. It is hard to know when your parents need help because, most of the time, they will not ask for it. They don't want to be a burden or feel as if they're imposing. They also may have trouble admitting that they are no longer self-sufficient or actually need the assistance. Thus, before jumping in you need to consider the following:

- How much help is needed?
- Siblings: Do you divide and conquer? Geography is a factor when most are not in the same location or town.

- What are the costs involved both financially and temporally?
- What type of care is needed? Long term or short term? Full time or just a few hours a day?
- Do they have any Long Term Care Insurance to cover the expenses?

This is an issue discussed with many of my clients. If they are young enough, the children can purchase long-term care for the parents. They say, "I am responsible anyway, so I would like to hedge my expenses and plan ahead." This makes perfect sense as you can structure this as part of your budget and work to create a financial safety net in this area of your life.

Will they Qualify for Long Term Care?

Knowing that there is a great likelihood of long term care needed, we should begin to understand if your loved ones will even qualify for long term care. If they are already in need of care or have any symptoms of Alzheimer's, memory loss, and/or dementia, then the answer is "no." But, if there are no present medical conditions, there is a high likelihood an insurance company will be willing to take them on and offer coverage for long-term care if and when there is a need. However, if the current diagnosis is not a positive one, here are some examples of how my clients and I have handled this:

24-Hour Care in the Home. My grandmother had a bit of all of the above: Alzheimer's, memory loss, and dementia. In fact, it runs in the family. She needed 24-hour care. She did not want to leave the house and was otherwise physically healthy. But her mind was going quickly and we needed to implement a plan. One of the first steps is to determine the type of care needed. Is skilled or non-skilled care required? In her case it was non-skilled. We had two women, each taking a twelve-hour shift. They would visit her house and cook, clean, shop, and help her to get washed and dressed. They were also there as companions. Their most important duty was to make sure she didn't leave the stove on or do anything to unintentionally hurt herself. My family took out a home equity loan to pay for 24-hour care. This might also be accomplished with a reverse mortgage.

Bring Your Parent In House. I had one client who brought her mom to live with her in her home. She had to build an addition on to the house. She used her mom's money to do this, which she worried might cause sibling issues. But she consulted an elder care attorney before proceeding to equalize the estate and offset the initial expense. It paid great dividends in peace of mind to know her mother was safe and sound in the next room.

Part Time Care. Another client made up the shortfall for her parents. She brought in caregivers for a few hours each day. They would have sibling meetings and all would equally chip in to take care of mom and dad. They also reached out to the senior center and used Meals on Wheels to help with making sure mom and dad were eating properly. Strong communication and putting a plan in place did the trick to create a healthy environment for their loved ones.

Money Queen Fact: Of women who have or plan to take time out of the workforce to be a caregiver, 74% believe that it will negatively impact their ability to save for retirement.[32]

Continuing Care Retirement Communities (CCRC). One of my clients opted for a CCRC. They are part independent living, part assisted living, and part skilled nursing home. CCRC's offer a tiered approach to the aging process, accommodating their residents' changing needs. Upon entering, healthy adults can reside independently in single-family homes, apartments, or condominiums. When assistance with everyday activities becomes necessary, they can move into assisted living or nursing care facilities. These typically work by selling the home and then buying into the community. You will get some money refunded at death, so it might be considered an asset depending on which contract you use. This is an expensive option, but it offers some of the best amenities. CCRC's require a hefty entrance fee, as well as monthly charges. Entrance fees can range from $100,000 to $1 million, and are an upfront sum to prepay for care, as well as to provide the facility with money to operate. Monthly charges can range from $3,000 to $5,000, but may increase as needs change.

Nursing Homes. The process of choosing one that is right for your parents is overwhelming. But the AARP is a good place to start. They offer good resources on nursing homes as well as information to help learn the system. You can go to: *http://assets.aarp.org/external_sites/ caregiving/options/ nursing_home_system.html.* The government also offers help. You can compare Medicaid and Medicare via websites like: *http://www.medicare.gov/nursinghomecompare/About/What-Is-NHC. html.* The "U.S. News and World Report" also ranks facilities at this website: *http://health.usnews.com/best-nursing-homes.*

You may use one of these options or a combination of the above. Every woman wants the best care for her parents. Cost and paying for this is a major factor to be considered. Remember that unless you are on Medicaid, Medicare does not cover these costs. But you can get short-term coverage by Medicare if you are expected to recover. I have seen clients spend their entire life savings at the end of their life to pay for these costs. Long Term Care, either traditional or asset based, is a good option to have. If you are going to pay for long-term care for your parents, you are either protecting your inheritance or potentially lowering your costs if you plan to pay for them. All of these are difficult life decisions we have to make. Our parents cared for us, now it is our time to return the favor.

With that in mind, consider that there is a high likelihood that you will be responsible, in some form or another, for some part of the required care for your loved ones as they age. The goal is to do everything you can to help them age gracefully and provide the support and ultimately, the medical care they may need. Life is unpredictable, so assume the worst and start the planning and saving process early on to ensure you are well prepared when difficult times approach.

Chapter 9

YOUR SMOOTH 60'S (AND BEYOND): A TIME TO CELEBRATE

Retirement

What does retirement mean to you? Does it mean financial freedom? Does it mean you never have to work again? Is it time to travel the world? Does it mean you get to spend all your time on your passions? Whatever the case may be, it means different things to different people. It used to be a rite of passage in the United States. Now, it is a goal for which we should all strive.

In the 1970's, the majority of retirement plans were defined benefit plans also known as pension plans. This is where you were guaranteed a dollar amount at retirement and the employer had all the risk. As the tax code changed, a shift began where employers began to change from defined benefit plans to defined contribution plans. Defined contribution plans are most commonly 401(k)'s, 403(b)'s and 457 plans. These types of plans require that the participants in the plan be responsible for investing in their own retirement plan to suit their risk tolerance and retirement needs, shifting that element of responsibility away from the employer. With social security only providing a fraction of living expenses, and considering factors such as inflation, those looking to retire in the future now have much more to plan for than retirees of the past.

Money Queen Fact: Social security replaces
only about 40% of a workers' prior wages.[33]

Successfully living your retirement dream is no longer as simple as "work for the same company for 30 years and receive a pension." It actually requires prudent financial planning.

There is an important emotional and psychological aspect to retirement as well. With retirement, some people embrace the opportunity of free time to do all the things they've always wanted to do. However, many people enjoy their work and it gives them purpose. So it is important to consider the most effective balance for you and your desires and needs. Retirement should be fulfilling and enjoyable. It is the culmination of all you have done to this point.

I have seen a few clients in my life struggle with not knowing what to do in retirement. It is also difficult for some married couples because the dynamic changes when both spouses are home full time. Imagine what your life will look like in retirement. What do you want it to be? Once you've figured that out, you will need a plan to get there. There's no better time to act than now.

Money Queen Facts: While both men and women are under saved for their retirements, the women polled had saved less than men—with a median retirement savings accumulated to date of $20,000 for women surveyed versus $25,000 for men.[34]

Another important question to ask prior to retirement is this: What does our money mean to us? It's not just a paycheck or a return on investment…it's more about what our money can do. Your thoughts may be something similar to the life goals I hear from clients every day:

- I can retire at 60
- I will buy a second house
- Once a year, I will take my grandchildren to Disney World

Tangible goals are what keep us on task when saving and planning. But, what happens when an objective has been met, or when positivity begins to reign again in the market?

These are the times we must be most diligent by reevaluating our goals, reviewing our processes with a trusted advisor, and ensuring that we stay on course. It's *not* a time to start experimenting with what you've earned. Rather, it is a time to protect what you've gained.

When the market is moving up, it can be easy to see opportunities for increased revenue. However, responsible planning means that you maintain focus on individual goals, not just investments and arbitrary numbers. For example, let's look again at the concept of the use of financial score cards to track performance. After devising a long-term strategy to ensure that enough funds will be available for you to meet various life goals at the time of retirement, revisiting that scorecard to track progress is vital. Just like saving is fluid, so is retirement. What works on day one may not work in year five.

Now, let's say that score reveals to you and your financial advisor that based on your savings and habits, you won't run out of money. It may feel as though a new freedom has been offered, but in fact, you've met a very specific and important benchmark of which you now must serve as steward.

At this point in your financial life, unnecessary risks are just that: unnecessary and dangerous. Avoid chasing stock performances looking for double-digit returns or looking for ways to capitalize on a well-performing index. Instead, you'd do better to protect your assets by setting new goals and objectives, and always define what your money means to you because even that definition shifts with time.

The bottom line is that the results of our investments shouldn't be looked at as numbers, but as what those dollars truly mean. To find financial freedom is not just to achieve, but to maintain the peace of mind that comes with the ability to afford a new home, retire at a certain age, or take your grandkids to Disney's Magic Kingdom every year. It's important to protect ourselves, as the market inevitably rises and falls, with a long-term strategy that guides us through storms as well as doldrums.

The 4% Rule has long been the benchmark for retirees managing their finances, representing a "safe rate" that allows for withdrawals while still ensuring a steady stream of revenue for a number of years. It's a tool that financial planners have used for decades to help their clients, and it arose from one of the most frequently asked questions we hear: *"How much money can we spend and still be okay?"*

However, like pensions and social security, things that were once set in stone are more fluid in today's economy. That percentage was calculated in the 1990's when portfolios were earning about 8%. That's just not the case anymore. Today, portfolios generally earn much less, about 3.5% to 4%, and stocks are high-priced, which has been linked to below-average future performance. That's all in addition to the fact that the economic climate we now live in is unlike anything our country has ever seen.

Money Queen Fact: Of the women who expect to rely on Social Security when they retire, only 14% have "a great deal" of understanding.[35]

The 4% Rule is a common rule used by financial planners for determining retirement income. It states that if you only withdraw 4% of your portfolio to live on, you should not run out of money! The 4% Rule is a great place to start, but getting a handle on cash flow in the retirement years is much more important than any rule. Everyone is different, and we all need to know what we're saving as well as what we're spending, what our risk tolerance is, when we hope to retire, and how much we hope to leave to our heirs, among other concerns.

The more you begin to pay attention and understand your own portfolio, the easier it is to make better, more informed decisions, and manage your annual Personal Withdrawal Rate (PWR). Markets go up and down, inflation skyrockets, better-than-expected promotions arise, and grandkids change everything. As life rises and falls, so must your PWR.

With a financial plan in place and some professional guidance, withdrawals can be made in the most tax efficient way from year-to-year to conform to the life transitions we experience. The only 'rules' are to stay consistent, diligent, and realistic.

Planning for a Curve Ball

It's important to be prepared in life. That is really the backbone of this entire book. Proper preparation can position you to avoid many of life's financial pitfalls. Whether it is making checklists, over packing, or planning far in advance, having a game plan is always a good idea. But even the best-laid plans don't always work out the way you want them to: This creates anxiety for Designer Bag Ladies. The key is in how you handle it.

There's no denying that I like to plan. I am a Financial Planner, after all. For every client meeting I have, I create an agenda. I plan out the meeting, prepare the necessary documentation and contact the appropriate parties. But every now and then I get thrown a curve ball. Should I stick to my plan? Or should I embrace the change in direction? Embrace it, of course.

I tell my clients to embrace change if they need to. Even though it's on a much smaller scale, why wouldn't I listen to my own advice? Things change. Plans don't work out the way you want. But instead of resisting the change, it's important to embrace it and go with the flow. Good things may happen!

Recently, I had a client come in and throw me a curve ball. Instead of discussing estate planning and annuities, she wanted to talk about her home, and, more specifically, what she wanted to do to it. A few years back, she and her husband purchased a home in a gated community for $400,000. It's a lovely home, but she wanted to add another room for her crafts—to the tune of $30,000. Now, here's the clincher: Her home was only worth $275,000 in today's market. Despite being completely prepared, having already met with an architect and securing a Home Equity Loan, she wasn't prepared for the reality of the situation.

Living in a gated community, there are restrictions. She couldn't build the addition without first going through the community association and the town for permits. And she could be fined if she decided to host classes out of her new craft room.

Does it make financial sense? It didn't. But if it were something she truly wanted, then I wasn't going to stop her. But I did throw her a curve ball of my own. I told her to buy a new house that already has an extra room for her crafts and rent out her current home for a year.

The math showed that by renting the house, they could then write off the $125,000 loss on their taxes the next year. Did she embrace the change? Of course she did. In that same meeting, her husband, who has Parkinson's disease, also brought up another question I wasn't expecting. He asked if he should retire early, or go on disability? This was another curve ball with a simple answer.

Because he had been paying for disability insurance out of his own pocket, he was able to take long-term disability leave and receive 70% of his income, all tax-free. Not only did he not have to retire early, he was also able to take advantage of the benefits he had been paying for years on end.

So the next time you're thrown a curve ball that changes your plans, don't worry about it. Embrace the change because you never know when a different plan will work out better than the one you envisioned. It is difficult to plan for curve balls because you never know how quickly they will come and from what direction they will travel. This is part of the motivation to have a trusted advisor or financial advocate who knows your situation and can speak to you and come up with advice and solutions when obstacles present themselves. For my clients, we have regular meetings to review financial stability and ability to withstand difficult and unexpected circumstances.

My Heart Will Go On

I often make the analogy between financial planning and following a road map. Sometimes, though, life circumstances can be so disruptive that we can't even see the road before us, let alone follow the path ahead. At these times, it helps to look at your life not as a road, but a tree: One with strong roots, and the ability to branch off into countless directions.

Losing a spouse is one of these times. Unfortunately, it's something that can happen to couples young and old, and while every widow will face a different set of challenges, the one trait shared by everyone is extreme grief. No one wants to think about it or even discuss it, but the truth is that us women are likely to outlive our male counterparts. So there is a high likelihood we will have to deal with the passing of our significant other. When taking those first difficult steps forward after a death, the analogy of a tree is helpful because it illustrates a life that grew in one direction for some time, which now must adapt to a change in the environment without toppling over.

Money Queen Fact: Between ages 75 and 84, more than 60% of women are single or widowed. That number jumps to 87% after age 85.[36]

It also helps people find the answers to not just, *"Where do I go next?"* but also, *"What's important to me?"* by reminding them of the seeds that first made that tree grow: family, security, and legacy to name just a few. Clear-mindedness takes on additional importance when we think about the changes a widow might need to make at this point in her life. Not only has she become solely responsible for her finances, her monthly income may change, as might her arrangements, work schedule, and more.

I recommend specialized counseling or support groups to all of my widowed clients above all else. Financial planning is about the future, and new widows are most focused on getting through each day, as they should be. Without addressing grief and its many stages first, it's virtually impossible to separate emotion from financial decision-making.

When ready, one of the first decisions a widow can make, is what kind of professional is her ideal financial advocate. It's important to identify who is going to offer the highest comfort level. It may not be her late partner's financial planner or the first advisor she interviews, and it may or may not be a woman. Some widows choose to bring a trusted family member with them to preliminary meetings as well. Regardless of your path, ensure you are thinking with your best interests in mind and not simply the overwhelming emotions you may initially experience. If that means you need to take some time away or create a buffer before you begin handling these important issues, rest assured that is normal. But eventually you will have to recognize the importance of tying up the loose ends.

The work to be done is undeniable and daunting, but there are resources to help a widow through one of the most difficult times in her life. For example, I have what I call a "widows package." It has lots of worksheets and a tree where you get to create what you want your life to look like now. It takes time to do this and we do it in baby steps. But it starts the momentum towards financial recovery. Tools like these, paired with a team of professionals trained to navigate tough terrain, can ultimately be the difference between a tree that bends to the wind and one that stands tall in a new light.

The first question that comes to mind for most widows and widowers when "we" becomes "me," is: *what happens next?* I tell everyone the same thing: The first step is to grieve; the next step is to plan. The most important thing one can do is grieve, and for as long as they need to. The mourning process can last weeks, months, and even years, but regardless of the time it takes, it is necessary to process your emotions before even thinking about your finances.

Only when you are finally ready to move forward can you delve into your finances. This process forces you to ask yourself challenging questions you may not want to answer, but that are necessary to set yourself up for the future. Consider the following questions as valuable initial "feelers" as you begin the process of rebuilding and putting the pieces back together:

- **Should you sell your home?** You may have years of memories in the home you shared with your spouse, which can make this a difficult decision. It's important to assess whether or not you are able to afford the home, especially if you never planned to live there during retirement.

- **Do you have enough money that you don't have to work?** No one wants to work when they should be retired. This is the perfect time to assess your income and decide how much money you need to save each month, as well as how much you can spend. Budgets are your friend. If you do not have enough in the bank, begin the process of re-entry into the workforce and find a job that is both satisfying and financially helpful. The best part is that re-entry may keep you busy and keep your mind off of the difficult personal circumstances with which you are dealing.

- **If you do have money, what should you do with it?** If you did receive money, whether it was from insurance, a retirement fund, or from simply planning, you need to decide now what do with it. Sure, you can put it in the bank or under a mattress, or you can trust a financial advisor to turn it into your income. But make a decision and stick with it.

- **Are you going to be a burden to your family?** It sounds awful, but you need to consider your family as well. Will you need life insurance, long-term care, or estate planning? Planning for grandkids and kids at this stage is also crucial. You will surely want to support them with fun activities, vacations, and birthday gifts. So ensure you are financially capable of doing so.

Moving on from your past and towards your future is never easy, especially when you try to do it on your own. There are ways to save money on your own, such as CD's and Treasury Bills, but options like that don't yield as much as they used to and simply aren't as reliable as finding a good financial advisor.

Making the Right Pick for You

At this point, we have covered an enormous amount of information regarding the various help financial advisors can offer. But more importantly, the goal of this book was to help you, as you journey through your life, to make smart and informed financial decisions. It is not easy. If it were, everyone would be financially secure. But through a little bit of dedication, determination, and education, it is within reach. If you do decide to go the route of finding a financial advisor, remember to interview potential candidates— don't just go with the first person you meet. After all, you will entrust this person with your money, so you need to trust them. Here are some questions to ask when you're interviewing a potential advisor:

- What experience do you have?
- What are your qualifications?
- What services do you offer?
- What is your approach?
- What types of clients do you work with?
- Will you be the only financial planner I would work with?
- How do I pay?
- How much do you charge?
- Can anyone besides me benefit from your recommendations?

Remember, too, when someone is able to instill a sense of comfort, it often means they're on your side. And we all need people on our side. Life can be overwhelming at times. It can throw you off course and place plenty of obstacles right in your path. But with the correct team of advisors, you can find yourself better prepared to handle what lies ahead.

Leaving an Inheritance

As we come to an end, the last and most appropriate area of discussion is within the category of inheritance. At death, all those things you have compiled over the years have to go somewhere. You can't take them with you, and most funeral houses won't let you bury them by your side. So to ensure they can find new homes and do not cause an enormous family rift, let's discuss how to plan for this inevitable outcome. More than $15 trillion will be transferred to the next generation between 2007 and 2026. Thus, you better have a plan designating where everything will go.

Money Queen Fact: The average annual income for an elderly man ($24,300) is almost 75% higher than an elderly woman's annual income ($14,000).[37]

When most estate planning attorneys write trusts, they put in the ages of 25, 35, 45 and some even start at 35, 45, and 55. They have been doing it this way for decades. They want to make sure the children are *not* children, but rather that they are mature and not relying on this money. The goal is to provide financial security for your loved ones later in life when they are mature enough to handle the responsibility.

Leaving a Legacy: What and When to Communicate With Your Beneficiaries

With this mind, let's chat about creating your estate plan. When beginning to develop your estate plan, the first step is to identify what your goals are, beginning with how much money you want to leave and to whom you'd like to be the beneficiaries of those assets. After you've quantified your goal and designed a tax efficient distribution plan with your estate-planning attorney, the next question becomes: "what and when should I tell my heirs?"

When it comes to talking about money, some clients are more open than others. Some may have a specific reason why they want to talk about it, where as others may not feel it's appropriate until after they're gone. Based on my experience, every client is different, and you are going to hear varying opinions on the subject. The information you choose to share is completely dependent upon the circumstances in your own life and financial situation. But to this end, consider the following questions as you consider the best way to deal with the sensitive nature of death and money:

- How comfortable are you talking about money?
- Are the recipients of your estate mature enough to understand what you are telling them?
- Are the recipients of your estate mature enough to handle the legacy you're leaving?
- Do you believe your heirs need any financial education prior to receiving their share of your estate?
- Is there any jealousy or bad blood between the various respective heirs?
- Could the way you divided your estate create tension between the respective heirs after you're gone, particularly if discussed in advance?

These are all important questions you should be asking yourself during the estate planning process, and I would suggest consulting with your team of advisors prior to discussing or sharing any information with your heirs. At the end of the day, you need to do what makes the most sense for you and your family's needs.

Charity

There will probably be a time when you and your family will have a conversation about donating or giving some of your hard-earned money to charity. You may feel it is very important to set-aside some portion of your net worth as you earn and your success grows. That can be done during the course of your life as well as after your life ends. The options are endless and I have worked closely with clients to ensure that charitable contributions play an important role in financial planning. This may seem one like one more daunting task under the umbrella of planning. You may think: *If I need to make these checks and balances for my own future, then how can I possibly fit in giving to the causes I care about?*

The good news is you can. You may need to give smaller amounts at first, but there are a myriad of ways to fit philanthropy into your financial picture, and not all of them amount to simply writing out a check. In fact, charitable planning can be—dare I say it—fun, in that you can get creative, find out what works best for you, and over time see the difference your giving can make to others.

Money Queen Fact: Three out of five women over 65 cannot afford to cover their basic needs.[38]

What's more, many charitable giving plans can also improve the health of your own bottom line. U.S. tax laws provide significant incentives to individuals who voluntarily support their community and society with charitable gifts. They make it possible to increase charitable gifts, your own lifetime benefits, and benefits to heirs, while also reducing personal taxes. They can also reduce capital gains, and create an income stream for life when blended into your overall financial planning picture. This is because charitable planning diversifies assets without creating an immediate tax liability, and also provides the person who gives both income and control over the funds.

If you're going to potentially give to a charitable organization (or many), in addition to saving for children or other family, there are also a number of vehicles for the funds you've chosen to set aside. All of these avenues have major pluses; it's simply a matter of what's best for you and your personal situation.

For example, let's use Charitable Remainder Trusts (CRTs) to illustrate some of the benefits. A Charitable Remainder Trust (CRT) is a "split interest trust" that provides income for life (or for a term of years) to one or more income beneficiaries. After the term expires or the income beneficiaries pass away, the trust assets pass to one or more charitable beneficiaries. When you contribute cash or assets to a CRT, you are generally entitled to an income tax charitable deduction.

Therefore, if a woman in her seventies, who owns several stocks worth $100,000 and sees dividends of about $2,000 per year, decides to give these stocks to a charitable remainder annuity trust, she will qualify for a partial income tax deduction of more than $50,000, receive $5,000 a year instead of $2,000, and provide a future gift to a qualified charitable organization. Charitable donations are simply a way to make a difference while simultaneously saving real dollars through tax benefits. With this in mind, here are a few more options to consider with your financial advisor:

- **Charitable Lead Trust.** A trust that pays a charity income from a donated asset for a set number of years, after which time the principal goes to the donor's beneficiaries with reduced estate or gift taxes.
- **Private Foundation Gifts.** Private foundations are charitable organizations that do not qualify as public charities. Often, they're nonprofits that were established with funds from a

single source or specific sources, such as family or corporate money. Although contributions to private foundations technically are tax deductible, many of these nonprofits do not accept donations. Instead, private foundations usually invest their principal funding, and then distribute the income from investments for charitable purposes.

- **Charitable Gift Annuity.** A Charitable Gift Annuity involves a contract between a donor and a charity, whereby the donor transfers cash or property to the charity in exchange for a partial tax deduction and a lifetime stream of annual income from the charity. When the donor dies, the charity keeps the gift.
- **Charitable Gift Fund.** Charitable gift funds are vehicles for giving that are established as charitable affiliates of for-profit financial institutions, such as banks and mutual fund companies. These funds are donor-advised funds. Therefore, distribution is made to nonprofit organizations at the advice of the donor, with final authority being the board of the charitable affiliate.

Using one of these vehicles, or another option discussed with your financial planner, people in varying life stages can add charitable contributions to their financial picture and create a benefit for themselves and their families at the same time. It's a win-win situation that's as responsible as it is generous.

Your Legacy

Much of our journey to this point has been centered on what you can do during your life. While it may not be something actively discussed while living, your legacy is a crucial topic to address and discuss. Legacy is a beautiful, yet equally complicated word. It is your history, your past and the memory that others will attribute to you. Your legacy is also what you leave behind for your loved ones when you're gone. In the famous book *Fahrenheit 451*, author Ray Bradbury writes, "Everyone must leave something behind when he dies, my grandfather said. A child or a book or a painting or a house or a wall built or a pair of shoes made. Or a garden planted. Something your hand touched some way so your soul has somewhere to go when you die, and when people look at that tree or that flower you planted, you're there. It doesn't matter what you do, he said, so long as you change something from the way it was before you touched it into something that's like you after you take your hands away. The difference between the man who just cuts lawns and a real gardener is in the touching, he said. The lawn-cutter might just as well not have been there at all; the gardener will be there a lifetime."

Money Queen Fact: *The average woman can expect to live to 80.1 years old. Men live an average of 74.8 years.*[39]

Your legacy is an end-of-life factor that is completely controlled by you—after all it is your life, so it is your choice how you want to be remembered. For most people, it can be a bit uncomfortable to think about what will happen when they're gone. They may not have come to terms with an illness or do not want to upset their loved ones, but regardless of the situation, it is important to think about your wishes ahead of time. When contemplating your legacy and what you want to leave behind, I always recommend that you ask yourself a few important questions.

- What do I want to leave behind? This is where finances come into play. You may wish to leave money, so planning ahead to save is critical. It is also important to determine if you wish to leave money in today's value, or plan ahead to adjust for inflation. For example, say you wish to leave your family $1 million. Now, you can leave them that amount, but the value of that $1 million will change over the course of the years, due to inflation. In 40 years, assuming an average 3.5% inflation, that $1 million is really $3.956 million.

- Who are you giving it to? As noted earlier, you may wish to leave money to a charity or organization. But more commonly, people wish to leave money behind for family members and loved ones. The choice is yours. If you decide to leave it to your family member, who in particular? A grandchild or great-grandchild? If so, this requires a generation-skipping trust. Most likely, you would like to leave as much as you can without enabling your family to become complacent and not work. Unfortunately, I have seen cases where the recipients just waited for their payments and did not become active within society. It is a sad situation when this occurs, so it is important to take steps to motivate your beneficiaries.

- Do you want to have strings attached? If you have a trust, you can still pull strings from beyond the grave. For example, if the recipient earns a graduate degree, they can be given a pre-determined amount of money, or if a grandchild faces any legal troubles, they can lose their inheritance automatically. This is what is great about trusts. It provides you the opportunity to control what your loved ones receive based on their behavior when you're not there.

- Do you want the money to last generations? How and when payments are made is up to you. There is the option for a lump-sum payment, or you can write the trust to schedule payments over time. Think about to whom the money is being gifted so you can ensure you set smart boundaries to mirror the exact situation.

- How do you wish to be remembered? Now, this aspect is less about money, and more about the other meaning of legacy—

your memory. Most people know how they want to be remembered when they pass. Some want to be remembered as caring and loving, some want to be remembered for their accomplishments, and others may want to be immortalized as the practical joker of their family. But no matter your wishes, the best thing you can do is plan ahead and let your loved ones know how you feel. Personally, I think that video and written legacies are a touching way to memorialize your life for your family. A great resource for this is *Five Wishes*, a little book that you can write in, which helps explain how you want to be remembered, how you want to be treated, and what you want to pass on. *Five Wishes* also serves as a healthcare proxy to help determine medical treatments. And if you're into more reading, another great book is *The Ultimate Gift* by Jim Stovall. It is written to provoke thought, encourage discussion, and is a tool for families to teach valuable life lessons. Another great resource where people can share pictures and stories about their loved ones and keep their memories alive is www.legacy.com.

Remember that when all is said and done, it is the stories that keep your memory alive. How do *you* wish to be remembered?

Designer Bag Ladies Plan Now

Remember, Designer Bag Ladies are those women who are remarkably successful, but still carry enormous fears and concerns regarding their financial worth and stability. But they don't have to. In fact, they shouldn't. We see more and more of these successful women that can afford to live their dream lives. And they can simultaneously have the security for which they long. But it comes with a price. And that price is making good financial decisions as the money comes in. A Designer

Bag isn't cheap. In fact, it's pretty expensive. But it is a metaphor for life. Much like a happy life, it is coveted and if worked for, available for the taking.

So for all my Designer Bag Ladies—know that you are truly remarkable and can have it all. In fact, you should have it all. But it requires that you make smart decisions as early as your twenties. And then continue those sound decisions through your thirties, forties, fifties, sixties, and seventies. We are all part of the new definition of "working women" and can make our own rules and enjoy and celebrate our unique journeys.

Allen Saunders famously said, "Life is what happens when you are making other plans." For many of us, on a daily basis we take the time to plan. We plan meals, trips to the grocery store, dates, and pretty much anything and everything else. We live in a world of planners. But, for many of us, we refuse to plot our financial existence. Everything else is planned, but the financial backbone of our lives that actually supports everything is often swept under the rug. For those that don't sweep it under the rug, it is commonplace to at least delay proper planning. We put it off for tomorrow, justify the delay, or only put a few of the necessary pieces into place.

If nothing else, this book should open your eyes to the amazing opportunities available to you and your financial well-being. Creating financial stability does not happen overnight. It does take dedication and time, but is absolutely within reach for us all. Start small. Meet with a financial planner and discuss the most important pieces to immediately put into place. Then build on them, one day and one piece at a time. Remember that this is a team effort, and calls for your partner, children, friends, and loved ones' best efforts as well. Regardless of what you do today, life is going to happen tomorrow.

Money Queen Fact: 62% of women don't have a financial planner.[40]

Before you know it, life's milestones will begin to occur. College. Your first child. A new job. Paying for a wedding. Retirement. Loss of a loved one. Providing for the next generation. Each of these carry enormous financial burden but can also be prepared and planned for. Our journey together is coming to a close, but your journey to financial health and prosperity begins today. There is not a time too soon for you to begin. And if you feel it is too late, you are wrong. Catch up is simply part of the game. So long as you are moving one foot in front of the other and in the direction of your goals, you are doing great. We can all agree there is no downside to planning and financial well-being. It is an integral part of our lives. I am hopeful that this book has given each of you at least a few nuggets of wisdom that you can implement into your life and use to become a better planner.

Earlier, we spoke of legacies. My goal is that I will be remembered as someone who made the world a better place by building financial security for others. But I can only do so much. This journey starts from within and it starts with you. So take the time now to stand up and begin the process of putting one foot in front of the other. Because at the end of the day, the rest of your life is headed your way, whether you have planned for it or not.

ABOUT THE AUTHOR

 **Cary Carbonaro** is a Certified Financial Planner with an MBA in finance, and has over 25 years of experience in financial services. In 2014, she was named an Ambassador for the CFP Board, one of only 50 in the United States. She is a Managing Director of United Capital Financial Advisers, a Financial Life Management company.

Because of her credentials, Cary is frequently sought out for her expertise and has been quoted in a variety of well-known publications, including: *The Wall Street Journal, Newsday, New York Post, USA Today, The Street.com, Bloomberg, CNBC, Bankrate, Money Magazine, More Magazine, Kiplinger's and Investor's Business Daily*. She has also served as the *Orlando Sentinel's* "Money Matters Hotline" Expert. Cary has also been a guest on "The Today Show", CBS, Fox News, ABC, NPR and WPIX (NY) and has been a frequent contributor to PBS Nightly Business.

In addition to co-authoring the book *TIPS from the TOP: Targeted Advice from America 's Top Money Minds* (Alpha, 2003), she was also a contributor to *The Wealth Management Manual* and *Save Now or Die Trying.*

She currently serves as the Vice President of the Long Island chapter of Ellevate (formerly 85 Broads) a women's professional networking organization, and President of the South Lake (Florida) Community Foundation, Women's Giving Circle, which provides community based philanthropic support.

Cary was a CFP® instructor at Fordham University in New York and also taught Masters Level Marketing at The University of Phoenix.

She resides in both Florida and New York, and is a yoga instructor in her free time.

SOURCES

1 Analysis of U.S. Census data by Wider Opportunities for Women
2 "Women, Money and Power" Allianz Life Insurance Study
3 "Women, Money and Power" Allianz Life Insurance Study
4 What Women Need to Know About Retirement: A joint project of the Heinz Family Philanthropies and the Women's Institute for a Secure Retirement
5 Financial Experience &Behaviors Among Women, 2010–2011 Prudential Research Study (article breaking it down here).
6 "Women, Money and Power" Allianz Life Insurance Study and CFP Board
7 What Women Need to Know About Retirement: A joint project of the Heinz Family Philanthropies and the Women's Institute for a Secure Retirement
8 Analysis of U.S. Census data by Wider Opportunities for Women

9   Financial Experience &Behaviors Among Women, 2010–2011 Prudential Research Study (article breaking it down here).

10 14th Annual Transamerica Retirement Survey of Workers (2014)

11 "Women, Money and Power" Allianz Life Insurance Study

12 14th Annual Transamerica Retirement Survey of Workers (2014)

13 *Time* magazine, "Women, Money and Power," 3/26/12.

14 *Time* magazine, "Women, Money and Power," 3/26/12.

15 http://www.forbes.com/sites/manishathakor/2011/02/16/shocking-statistics-on-women-retirement-3/

16 What Women Need to Know About Retirement: A joint project of the Heinz Family Philanthropies and the Women's Institute for a Secure Retiremen

17 14th Annual Transamerica Retirement Survey of Workers (2014)

18 Analysis of U.S. Census data by Wider Opportunities for Women

19 http://www.investopedia.com/financial-edge/0412/scary-statistics-about-retirement-for-women.aspx

20 http://www.investopedia.com/financial-edge/0412/scary-statistics-about-retirement-for-women.aspx

21 Financial Experience &Behaviors Among Women, 2010–2011 Prudential Research Study(article breaking it down here).

22 Financial Experience &Behaviors Among Women, 2010–2011 Prudential Research Study (article breaking it down here).

23 Financial Experience &Behaviors Among Women, 2010–2011 Prudential Research Study (article breaking it down here).

24 14th Annual Transamerica Retirement Survey of Workers (2014)

25 Analysis of U.S. Census data by Wider Opportunities for Women

26 What Women Need to Know About Retirement: A joint project of the Heinz Family Philanthropies and the Women's Institute for a Secure Retirement

27 What Women Need to Know About Retirement: A joint project of the Heinz Family Philanthropies and the Women's Institute for a Secure Retirement

28 14th Annual Transamerica Retirement Survey of Workers (2014)

29 http://www.forbes.com/sites/manishathakor/2011/02/16/shocking-statistics-on-women-retirement-3/

30 14th Annual Transamerica Retirement Survey of Workers (2014)

31 Allianz Insurance 2013 Women, Money and Power Study (Insights) and White Paper. (Article by MSN Money breaking it down here).

32 14th Annual Transamerica Retirement Survey of Workers (2014)

33 What Women Need to Know About Retirement: A joint project of the Heinz Family Philanthropies and the Women's Institute for a Secure Retirement

34 http://www.forbes.com/sites/manishathakor/2011/02/16/shocking-statistics-on-women-retirement-3/

35 http://www.investopedia.com/financial-edge/0412/scary-statistics-about-retirement-for-women.aspx

36 What Women Need to Know About Retirement: A joint project of the Heinz Family Philanthropies and the Women's Institute for a Secure Retirement

37 Analysis of U.S. Census data by Wider Opportunities for Women

38 Analysis of U.S. Census data by Wider Opportunities for Women

39 What Women Need to Know About Retirement: A joint project of the Heinz Family Philanthropies and the Women's Institute for a Secure Retirement

40 "Women, Money and Power" Allianz Life Insurance Study

41 CFP Board, Woman's Initiative Ressearch

CPSIA information can be obtained at www.ICGtesting.com
Printed in the USA
BVOW08s1411220216

437622BV00001B/1/P